SUPPORTING STUDENT LEARNING

CASE STUDIES, EXPERIENCE & PRACTICE FROM HIGHER EDUCATION

EDITED BY
GLENDA CROSLING & GRAHAM WEBB

First published in 2002

Kogan Page Limited
120 Pentonville Road
London N1 9JN
UK

Stylus Publishing Inc.
22883 Quicksilver Drive
Sterling VA 20166–2012
USA

British Library Cataloguing in Publication Data

A CIP record for this book is available from the British Library.

ISBN 0 7494 3535 6 (paperback)
ISBN 0 7494 3534 8 (hardback)

Typeset by Saxon Graphics Ltd, Derby
Printed and bound in Great Britain by Biddles Ltd, Guildford and King's Lynn
www.biddles.co.uk

CONTENTS

Contributors   *ix*

Introducing Student Learning Support   1
Glenda Crosling and Graham Webb

THE CASE STUDIES

Section 1: Relating to Students

1. **Mentoring Rosie** *Martha Bean*   17
    Mentoring students from different cultural, linguistic and
    socio-economic backgrounds

2. **The Heart and the Machine** *Janet Robbins*   25
    Assisting a female student who is struggling with learning to use
    computers

3. **Doing it Hard** *Ormond Simpson*   34
    A teacher deals with his own disapproval, strong emotions and
    judgemental attitudes while working with a student who has a past

4. **The Personal is the Professional** *Sonia Thompson*   41
    Supporting students from gay and lesbian groups which have
    traditionally been discriminated against

5. **Intercultural Inexperience** *Zhu Yunxia and Jacqueline Harrison*   49
    Intercultural miscommunication produced by body language

6. **Freedom to Fail** *Tanya Kantanis*   57
    Bridging the gap between adolescence and adulthood by
     encouraging students to accept responsibility for self-directed
    learning

7. **Lovely ShirLey** *Anonymous*   64
   Social and emotional miscommunication involving a student
   from a culturally-diverse background and the medium of e-mail

8. **Dilemma for Two** *Eira Makepeace*   72
   Finding a way through a complex case involving legal, ethical,
   academic, regulatory, educational and psychological issues

Section 2: Developing Students' Academic Skills

9. **I Can Only Do it With Aspirin** *Linda Galligan*   81
   Preparing 'non-mathematical' students for mathematics in
   nursing studies

10. **Accounting?: I Can Do That** *Linda Forson*   88
    Helping first-year students survive a course with a very high
    failure rate

11. **What's Information Literacy?** *Dolene Rossi and Leone Hinton*   96
    Assisting beginning students to develop information literacy skills

12. **How Can We Reach Them?** *Esther Daborn and Bill Guariento*   104
    Integrating language and academic support in an undergraduate
    engineering course to help students develop English language
    and report writing skills

13. **Reading for Life** *Faridah Pawan and Sharon Pugh*   111
    Supporting students with English as a second language and other
    under-prepared readers to acquire confidence, flexibility and
    strategic approaches to reading and learning from texts

14. **Back on Course – But ...** *Vanessa Charter*   119
    Assisting a university student with dyslexia

15. **Barriers or Bridges?** *Daniel Granger*   126
    Supporting students whose ethnic and socio-economic
    backgrounds or circumstances have not prepared them for
    higher education

16. **Taking the Initiative: From Academic Survival to Academic
    Success** *John Morley*   134
    Exploring the attitudes, strategies and skills developed by an
    overseas postgraduate student who starts with inadequate English
    proficiency but who achieves outstanding academic success

Section 3: Working with Staff

17. **Letter of the Law** *Colin Beasley* 145
Supporting first-year commerce students from non-English
speaking backgrounds with the language and discourse of law

18. **Academic Friend or Foe?** *Monique Osborn* 153
Entering a difficult academic environment and developing
relationships with teachers in order to affect change

19. **Generalizing the Generic** *Glenda Crosling and Alan Farley* 162
Adjusting the curriculum of a large business faculty to ensure the
development of students' generic skills.

20. **The Golden Triangle** *Phillipa Ferst* 170
Learning support staff balancing the triangular relationship
between themselves, students and subject tutors

Conclusion

21. **Dimensions of Sstudent Learning Support** *Glenda Crosling
and Graham Webb* 179

Further reading 187

Index 193

CONTRIBUTORS

Martha Bean was Associate Professor of Linguistics and Language Development at San José State University, California, USA. She died several months before the publication of this book.

Colin J Beasley is Lecturer in English as a second language in the Teaching and Learning Centre, Murdoch University, Perth, Western Australia. (e-mail: cbeasley@cleo.murdoch.edu.au)

Vanessa Charter is Education and Training Consultant at the Nottinghamshire Dyslexia Association, Nottingham, UK. (e-mail: vanessa.charter@theNDA.fsnet.co.uk)

Glenda Crosling is responsible for the Faculty of Business and Economics Language and Learning Services program at Monash University (Clayton), Australia, and is Faculty Transition and Generic Skills Adviser. (e-mail: glenda.crosling@celts.monash.edu.au)

Esther Daborn is Lecturer at the EFL Unit, University of Glasgow, UK. (e-mail: E.Daborn@efl.arts.gla.ac.uk)

Alan Farley is Associate Dean (Undergraduate Teaching) and Head of the Department of Accounting and Finance in the Faculty of Business and Economics at Monash University, Clayton, Victoria, Australia. (e-mail: alan.farley@buseco.monash.edu.au)

Phillipa Ferst is Learning Support Tutor at Canterbury Christ Church University College, Canterbury, Kent, England. (e-mail: pjf1@canterbury.ac.uk)

Linda Forson is Project Manager Academic Development at Technikon Southern Africa, South Africa. (e-mail: lforson@tsa.ac.za)

Linda Galligan is in the Office of Preparatory and Continuing Studies at the University of Southern Queensland, Toowoomba, Queensland, Australia. (e-mail:galligan@usq.edu.au)

Daniel Granger is Director of Distributed Learning and Extended Education at California State University Monterey Bay, Seaside, California. (e-mail: dan_granger@csumb.edu)

Bill Guariento works at the EFL Unit, University of Glasgow, UK. (e-mail:W.Guariento@efl.arts.gla.ac.uk)

Jacqueline M Harrison is Head of the School of Communication at UNITEC Institute of Technology in Auckland, NZ. (e-mail: jharrison@unitec.ac.nz)

Leone Hinton is Teaching Scholar in the Division of Teaching and Learning Services at Central Queensland University, Rockhampton Queensland, Australia. (e-mail: l.hinton@cqu.edu.au)

Tanya Kantanis is Coordinator of the Monash Transition Program at Monash University, Clayton, Victoria, Australia. (e-mail: tanya.kantanis@adm.monash.edu.au)

Eira Makepeace is Head of the Centre for Student Affairs at the University of the West of England, UK. (e-mail: Eira.Makepeace@uwe.ac.uk)

John Morley works at the University of Manchester, where he teaches academic English and provides tutorial support for international students. (e-mail: john.morley@man.ac.uk)

Monique Osborn is an academic member of the Language and Learning Services Unit, Monash University, Gippsland Campus, Victoria, Australia. (e-mail: Monique.Osborn@education.monash.edu.au)

Faridah Pawan is Assistant Professor in the Language Education Department at Indiana University, Bloomington, USA. (e-mail: fpawan@indiana.edu)

Sharon Pugh is Associate Professor of Language Education at Indiana University, USA (e-mail pughs@indiana.edu)

Janet Robbins works at the Academic Skills and Learning Centre, Australian National University, Canberra, ACT, Australia.
(e-mail: Janet.Robbins@anu.edu.au)

Dolene Rossi is in the School of Nursing and Health Studies at Central Queensland University, Rockhampton, Queensland, Australia.
(e-mail: d.rossi@cqu.edu.au)

Ormond Simpson is Director of the UK Open University Centre for Educational Guidance and Student Support.
(e-mail: o.p.simpson@open.ac.uk)

Sonia Thompson works in Student Services at Sheffield Hallam University in the UK.
(e-mail: s.thompson@shu.ac.uk)

Graham Webb is Professor and Director at the Centre for Higher Education Quality at Monash University, Melbourne, Victoria, Australia.
(e-mail: Graham.Webb@adm.monash.edu.au)

Zhu Yunxia is Associate Professor in the School of Communication at UNITEC, Auckland, New Zealand.
(e-mail: zyunxia@unitec.ac.nz)

INTRODUCING STUDENT LEARNING SUPPORT

Glenda Crosling and Graham Webb

If they can't make it at first year level, they shouldn't be at university.

You will come across these words, spoken by a senior academic, later in this book (Forson, Chapter 11). You may have heard people say the same kind of thing or you may have expressed similar concerns yourself. Lying behind such concerns are dramatic changes which have seen higher education move from an elite to a mass system. Not only are there now many more students in higher education, but they come from far more diverse backgrounds.

In accepting many more students, and students with considerable diversity and preparedness for higher education study, comes the question of how they can be supported to succeed. One approach is to deny any special responsibility on the part of an institution to help students: as the quote above dramatically expressed, if they struggle, 'they shouldn't be at university'. However, most institutions recognize that this leads to unacceptable wastage: wastage of resources in teaching and then failing students, not to mention wastage in terms of the hopes and aspirations of the students themselves. On the other hand, we know that failing students who access learning support programmes often become successful students. The area of student learning support has therefore become a recognized and important aspect of higher education and it is the focus of this book.

The case studies in this book describe points of crisis. Through the raw and often compelling experiences of staff and students in the cases, we hope that you will gain insight and illumination. The cases show not only how support programmes in various forms have contributed to students' successful progress with their studies, but also how staff have coped with the differing backgrounds, learning approaches and responses of students to their studies. These 'real-life' situations are therefore of interest to teaching staff, learning support staff, students, managers and all who have an interest in student learning.

The notion of support programmes for student learning in institutions of higher education is not new. In the United States for instance, such programmes have existed for more than a century (Stahl and King, 2000). However, the number and diversity of higher education students increased dramatically after World War Two and has accelerated rapidly over the last few decades. In the United Kingdom of the 1970s, the newly established Open University encouraged many adults into university study as part time or 'distance education' students. It was expected that by the year 2000, 30 per cent of 18 to 19-year-olds would attend higher education in the United Kingdom (Clark, 1995), and this figure has recently been boosted to 50 per cent. Similarly, in Australia in the late 1980s, the government introduced reforms that significantly increased the participation of under-represented groups (Dawkins, 1990).

This 'massification', the much larger numbers and increased diversity of students in higher education, has been a response to the need for a more highly trained workforce as modern societies and economies continue to increase in complexity (Altbach, 1999). This has led to institutions amalgamating and new universities being established, to educate students with skills and knowledge for the new circumstances.

Governments have also emphasized accountability, placing further pressure on student learning outcomes. Alongside this, employers expect graduate employees to be proficient in generic and lifelong learning skills. Other important factors include globalization and developments in electronic communication, meaning that institutions must now compete in the world market for students, who can study online and communicate electronically with teachers and fellow students. Adding to this, students need to be computer and information literate, and electronic communication and 'e' education have led to new approaches to teaching and learning. Significantly, in times when governments have reduced funding for higher education, students increasingly provide revenue as clients. This tends to mean that their needs are considered more fully.

The range of students from 'non-traditional' backgrounds includes:

- adults over the age of 25;
- part-time students;
- women (especially in non-traditional areas);
- students from rural backgrounds;
- students from ethnic and minority groups for whom English is a second language;
- international students;
- students with disabilities;
- students who are first generation in higher education.

Higher education courses are now more flexible in terms of location, and people can study, for example, in the workplace or even, as in a case in this volume, in prison. New areas of study such as computer science and the formal accreditation now required in areas such as nursing have brought in new groups of students. But diversity is not the only indicator of students who need academic support. Cutting across the different groups, it is now recognized that academic culture and its expectations and assumptions differ from those of secondary education and that *all* new students need to make what may be an uneasy transition.

WHAT IS STUDENT LEARNING SUPPORT?

Institutions have had to respond to the diversity of the student profile in a way that is 'both reciprocal and dynamic' (Dey and Hurtade, 1999: 300). Accordingly, the forms and focuses of support programmes vary widely. Overall though, the objectives of support programmes, often targeted at different student groups, can be summarized as:

- strategies to increase the participation and performance of disadvantaged or non-traditional students through tertiary awareness programmes;
- strategies for commencing and continuing students such as special admission, bridging and support programmes and units;
- strategies to analyse and address where cultures of disadvantage differ from the culture and traditions of higher education (Abbott-Chapman, Hughes and Wyld, 1992).

The overarching aim has been to make teaching materials and processes 'more relevant to the needs of disadvantaged students' (Dawkins, 1990: 3).

In the United States, approaches range from pre-course acquaintance and bridging programmes to supplemental instruction for courses where large numbers of students experience difficulty (McGrath and Townsend, 1996). These might focus on learning assistance, study strategies and developmental education, as well as reading, writing and mathematics skill development. There are 'writing across the curriculum' programmes and, for English as a second language students, programmes that respond to the different needs of second language resident students and international students (Harklau, Siegal and Losey, 1999). Individualized services such as online computer programs increasingly have potential as cost effective ways of assisting students (Maxwell, 2000).

In Australia, services generally aim to empower students so that they appreciate their own learning approaches, improve their communication skills and enhance their self-management (Candy, Crebert and O'Leary, 1994).

The three major types of learning intervention programme are:

- study skills programmes (eg lectures, workshops, handouts and resources on note taking, essay writing etc);
- programmes designed to change students' approach to learning (eg workshops to encourage a deep rather than a surface approach to learning);
- programmes designed to develop a reflective or metacognitive approach (eg encouraging reflection on learning and control over study) (Scouller, cited in McLean, Surtie, Elphinstone and Devlin, 1995).

Programmes may operate through work with individual students, resource collections, adjunct or supplemental programmes, in mainstream teaching programmes and through work with academic staff in designing curricula to include both content knowledge and generic skills. Many support programmes are contextualized so that academic skills development is embedded in the subject content (Candy, Crebert and O'Leary, 1994). Increasingly, learning support programmes and materials are offered online by most institutions (Webb, 2001).

In the United Kingdom,[1] the range of programmes includes higher education sampling programmes designed to attract mature age students, and credit and non-credit study skills units within the course. There are also individualized courses designed for students deemed to be at risk, and support for officially recognized dyslexic students.

WHAT WE KNOW ABOUT STUDENT LEARNING SUPPORT

The student learning field is wide, and this may account for the limited literature available of an integrative or general nature. On the other hand, there are many books available concerning best practice for support programme providers. In the following sections we attempt to identify some of the key dimensions relating to the field of student learning support.

Emotional and affective issues

The literature identifies the significance of affective as well as cognitive issues in supporting student learning. Learning supporters should therefore be equipped with understandings that include behavioural, cognitive, social learning, motivational and adult learning approaches, and be able to select and adapt these for particular cases. They should also be aware of the principles of higher education student development, sociolinguistics, metacognition, motivation and group dynamics. The importance of affective factors in learning support suggests that students need to be valued, regardless of their situation, and that learning supporters need to be authentic and empathic in their approach. This then suggests that they require listening and non-verbal skills, the ability to reflect before responding, to paraphrase a student's comments, and the skill of questioning. Relevant ethical issues also include confidentiality, care when intervening between student and tutor, and drawing the line between work with student learning and therapeutic counselling (Jones, Siraj-Blatchford and Ashcroft, 1998 (citing Rogers); Casazza and Silverman, 1996).

Programme diversity

Because of the diversity of the student population, programmes offered should be comprehensive, to cater for the range of issues and situations that arise for high risk students. Programmes should be proactive and offered early when 'at risk' students are vulnerable and could drop out of their studies. Students who are struggling do not always identify the existence of problems and often do not seek assistance. For instance, recently arrived international students may need early assistance to acculturate to the expectations of Western higher education study, including its emphasis on critical analysis (Ballard and Clanchy, 1991; Leki, 1992). Mature aged students who have been away from the educational system for some years may need to adapt to styles of teaching and learning that differ from their previous educational experiences. Students with learning disabilities may need ongoing support, as may students with English language difficulties. All of this points to the need for a diverse mix of support programme offerings.

Embedding support in mainstream courses

Support programmes need to embed their activities within broader academic preparation and global tasks. This is based on research that shows that decontextualized programmes are not effective in developing skills and understandings for academic study. Programmes should also emphasize higher order skills, use high quality communicative (rather than lecture) teaching, and complex, meaningful problems that encourage multiple thinking strategies, communication and collaboration among students (McGrath and Townsend, 1996). Evaluation processes should be integral to programmes as the basis for continuing achievement, improvement and innovation (Casazza and Silverman, 1996).

Transition to study in higher education

The literature suggests that the period of transition to higher education study is problematic for many students, regardless of their background. At this time, students should be encouraged and assisted to make friends with other students so that they can feel that they belong to their institution, faculty and/or department. They also need to become familiar with institutional structures and procedures, and teaching and learning processes, especially appreciating the independence expected of them in their own study. In this period, to encourage them to persist with their studies, students need to be motivated to perceive a purpose for their studies, and have some awareness of the academic standards of the their disciplines (Tinto, 1975; Pascarella and Terenzini, 1983; McInnes and James, 1995; Clark and Ramsey, 1990; Abbott-Chapman, Hughes and Wyld, 1992).

Studying in disciplines

Highly relevant to support and fundamental to academic literacy is the view commonly found in the literature that knowledge is structured in particular ways across the disciplines. Becher (1989), for example, explores the inter-connections of academic cultures and the nature of knowledge. For success in their disciplinary studies, students therefore need to adjust their general understandings of academic literacy to those of their specific discipline (Candlin, Bhatia and Hyland, cited in Candlin, Gollin, Plum, Spinks and Stuart-Smith, 1998). Some research investigates the characteristics of the discourse of particular disciplines such as medical English (Maher, 1986), legal English (Bhatia, 1993) and economics (Henderson, Dudley-Evans and Backhouse, 1993). Some texts, principally aimed at students, are useful for learning support providers too, as they investigate the assumptions and expectations of particular disciplines (eg Trimble, 1990: science and engi-neering; Riley,1991: law, especially in relation to ESL students; and Crosling and Murphy, 2000: law for business studies).

Writing in the disciplines

Writing takes on different forms across disciplinary fields, and the prevailing view is of writing as a social practice of the particular discipline, rather than a set of skills to be transferred to any setting (Lea and Stierer, 2000). To write suitably, the writer needs to appreciate, perhaps unconsciously, the processes and practices through which disciplinary knowledge is represented and upon which it is based, its position relative to other disciplines and the traditions underpinning the preference for certain genres and styles (Swales,

1990; Lea and Stierer, 2000). Swales' (1990) view is that although various genres pertain to all disciplines, these are emphasized differently across disciplines. Also relevant in the writing process is the writer's identity and how writers position themselves in relation to their readers (Ivanic, 1998). Hinds (1987) suggests that reader and writer responsibilities differ across cultures and that a writer in a Western culture needs to be explicit for the reader in direction and evaluation. If a reader-responsible position is adopted, the links would be left to the reader, and this may contravene the expectations of readers with Western expectations. Postgraduate students face an even more complex set of expectations in their research and thesis writing (Mauch and Birch, 1993; Ryan and Zuber-Skerritt, 1999; Swales and Feak, 1994).

Academic reading

As a further significant factor in academic literacy, appropriate academic reading can be seen as the basis for critical thinking, problem solving and effective expression (Pugh, Pawan and Antommarchi, 2000). It requires several abilities, including synthesizing, organizing and interpreting ideas, especially when an abundance of material is now available electronically. Again, academic reading should be seen as interactive in that the reader's experiences are harnessed in meaning construction (Pugh, Pawan and Antommarchi, 2000; Rosenblatt, 1994).

Summary

These then are some of the fundamental aspects of student learning support and areas in which there has been research. While the list is far from being comprehensive, these are also areas that we believe apply widely throughout student learning support. Further references concerning specific areas can be found in the Further Reading section of this book on page 185.

THE AUDIENCE

We hope that this book will provide insight into the experiences of student learning support providers, together with the staff and students with whom they work.

The book will be useful for several groups of staff in higher education:

- subject teachers who are concerned with academic achievement in relation to the varying background experience of students, and who wish to develop understanding of students from non-traditional backgrounds;

- academic staff developers who provide training and assist academic staff to develop insight into the nature of students in today's higher education system, and assist them to explore ways in which teaching and learning can be developed to cater for all students;
- student learning support staff who are interested in the many and various approaches to maximizing student learning and integrating learning support into mainstream teaching and learning.

THE CASES

The cases in this book follow the format of others in the series (Edwards, Smith and Webb, 2001; Murphy, Walker and Webb, 2001; Schwartz, Mennin and Webb, 2001; Schwartz and Webb, 1993; Schwartz and Webb, 2002), and we believe that there are strong links between the aspects of learning support identified in this book and the teaching and learning issues considered in the earlier books in the series, dealing with problem based learning, lecturing, online teaching, and learning and assessment. The present cases, like those in the earlier books, portray a wide spectrum of teaching and learning practice and provide powerful insights to the conditions determining the success or failure of learning support interventions.

The 20 cases have been developed by 24 higher education staff members from the United Kingdom, Australia, New Zealand, United States and South Africa. The areas and disciplines represented are diverse, including nursing, business and economics, communication, information technology, creative arts, education, community and youth studies, arts and engineering. The kinds of programmes considered in the cases are also diverse and include pre-course, mentoring and bridging programmes, those integrated with mainstream teaching, course-wide programmes, adjunct programmes running concurrently with subjects, supplemental instruction, intensive English programmes, and programmes designed for individual students. All the cases portray real events which were of such intensity that they forced the authors to reflect on their students' situations and needs. They caused the case writers to struggle with a situation and to devise strategies to support their students' learning and thus move forward. As real stories, the impact of the experience is evident in each case.

As with the other books in the series, each case is prefaced by an indication of the issue or issues raised and brief background information to set the scene for the events that follow. The case itself consists of two or more parts, each part being followed by questions for you to consider. This break for reflection occurs at a point of crisis, or where a decision is required. We ask you at this point to place yourself in the position of the author as you think about what should be done next, as well as what you think will actually happen next. You then find out what did actually happen, and after this we ask you to consider how the situation was handled, as well as some of the questions and issues raised by the case. The final section of the case is the author's discussion that raises questions such as:

- How well was the situation handled?
- What other options might there have been for dealing with it?
- What lessons did the author and the other parties to the incident learn from the experience?
- What lessons can you learn from the case?

We emphasize that there are no right or wrong answers to the crises and situations that arise in the cases. Furthermore, the authors' discussions in the final sections of the cases are not meant to be definitive, and we invite you to identify other views or issues that you see as arising from the situation, especially as you consider it in relation to your own context. Indeed, the main purpose of each case is to provoke your own thinking by inviting you to reflect on the suitability of the responses that were made, to apply these to your own situation and to consider their benefits and limitations.

In compiling the cases, we suggested to authors some areas that could be fruitful for development, and authors also made suggestions to us of other productive areas and issues. The result was a diverse set of cases which could be grouped in terms of student background or type of support programme.

Cases including student background include disadvantage in higher education because of socio-economic background (cases contributed by Granger, Bean, Forson), because of marginal group membership such as lesbian and gay students (Thompson), learning disabilities (Chapman), international or overseas, non-English speaking backgrounds, and postgraduate students (Morley, Zhu and Harrison, Pawan and Pugh, Anonymous, Beasley), women working with computers (Robbins), numeracy skills in a nursing course (Galligan), communication for engineering students (Daborn and Guariento).

Cases involving different types of support programmes include support at the individual level (Kantanis, Makepeace, Simpson, Ferst) in adjunct or supplemental classes (Beasley, Galligan, Forson) at the subject, course or policy level (Rossi and Hinton, Pawan and Pugh, Osborn, Crosling and Farley).

HOW TO USE THIS BOOK

As you read a case, we recommend that you 'play the game' and read only Part One. Following this, you should think about the story that is unfolding, what could be done next, what you think will happen next and what course of action *you* would follow. You should then repeat this procedure for Part Two (and others if necessary). The questions that have been provided at the end of each part will assist you with the framework for your interpretation and your response to what is going on in the case. As well as the specific questions for each case, you could ask yourself the following general questions.

At the end of Part One, ask:

- What is happening here?
- What factors could have contributed to the situation that is unfolding?
- How does the case author appear to see the case?
- What *other* interpretations might there be?
- How might the situation be handled?
- What consequences could be expected from possible actions?
- Given the nature of the participants, how will the situation probably be dealt with?

After the final part of the discussion, ask yourself:

- How well was the situation handled?
- What general issues are brought out by the case?
- What does the case and its issues mean for you?

We believe that this is the best way to gain the deepest insights from the case studies and discussions. At the same time, we suggest that you will also find it useful to discuss your impressions of the cases and the insights you gained from them with your colleagues. The cases can serve as useful training and development resources. In fact, the cases presented in the original book (Schwartz and Webb, 1993) were both the products of and the discussion materials for a series of group discussions in a faculty development programme.

We conclude the book with a list of further reading on supporting student learning. The readings include reference to general materials as well as information on issues raised in the particular cases. The case authors themselves have provided further readings that are particularly appropriate for the issues in their cases. The editors and the contributors also welcome enquiries from readers who would like more information and dialogue, and electronic mail addresses are provided for the editors and the case writers.

Finally, we hope that the cases and the reflections may provide you with greater insight into your own students, their learning and your teaching. We hope that they will stimulate you to think freshly and provide inspiration when practices that you have used in the past no longer seem to be as effective. The freshness, creativity and caring demonstrated throughout the cases is surely a lesson for us all.

Acknowledgement

We wish to thank and acknowledge Helen Lentell for her work on this book in the early stages, before she changed jobs and countries.

Notes

1 This overview was provided by Sonia Chapman, based on her wide experience in working in support programmes in Higher Education in the UK.

References

Abbott-Chapman, J, Hughes, P, and Wyld, C (1992) *Improving Access of Disadvantaged Youth to Higher Education,* Department of Employment, Education and Training, Australian Government Publishing Service, Canberra

Altbach, P (1999) Patterns in higher education development, in *American Higher Education in the Twenty-first Century,* ed P Altbach, R Berdahl and P Gumport, Johns Hopkins University Press, Baltimore

Ballard, B and Clanchy, J (1991) *Teaching Students from Overseas,* Longman Cheshire, Melbourne

Becher, T (1989) *Academic Tribes and Territories,* Society for Research into Higher Education and Open University Press, Buckingham

Bhatia, V (1993) *Analysing Genre: Language use in professional settings,* Longman, London

Candlin, C, Gollin, S, Plum, G, Spinks, S and Stuart-Smith, V (1998) *Researching Academic Literacies,* Department of Linguistics/National Centre for Language Teaching and Research/Centre for Language in Social Life, Macquarie University

Candy, P, Crebert, W and O'Leary, J (1994) *Developing Lifelong Learners Through Undergraduate Education,* National Board of Employment, Education and Training, Australian Government Publishing Service, Canberra

Casazza, M and Silverman, S (1996) *Learning Assistance and Developmental Education,* Jossey-Bass, San Francisco

Clark, E (1995) Open learning: educational opportunity a convenient solution to practical problems in higher education?, in *Flexible Learning Strategies in Higher and Further Education,* ed D Thomas, Cassell, London

Clark, E and Ramsay, W (1990) Problems of retention in tertiary education, *Education Research and Perspectives,* 17 (2), pp 47–59

Crosling, G and Murphy, H (2000) *How To Study Business Law,* 3rd edn, Butterworths, Sydney

Dawkins, J (1990) *A Fair Chance For All,* Australian Government Publishing Service for the Department of Employment, Education and Training and the National Board of Employment, Education and Training, Canberra

Dey, E and Hurtade, S (1999) Students, colleges and society: considering the interconnections, in *American Higher Education in the Twenty-first Century,* ed P Altbach, R Berdahl and P Gumport, Johns Hopkins University Press, Baltimore

Edwards, H, Smith, B and Webb, G (eds) (2001) *Lecturing: Case Studies, Experience, and Practice*, Kogan Page, London

Harklau, L, Siegal, M and Losey, K (1999) Linguistically diverse students and college writing: what is equitable and appropriate?, in *Generation 1.5 Meets College Composition*, ed L Harklau, M Losey and M Siegal, Lawrence Erlbaum, Mahwah, NJ

Henderson, W, Dudley-Evans, T and Backhouse, R (1993) *Economics and Language*, Routledge, London

Hinds, J (1987) Reader vs writer responsibility: a new typology, in *Writing Across Languages. Analysis of L2 texts*, eds U Connor and R Kaplan, Addison-Wesley, Reading

Ivanic, R (1998) *Writing and Identity*, John Benjamins, Amsterdam

Jones, M, Siraj-Blatchford, J and Ashcroft, K (1998) *Researching Academic Literacies*, Department of Linguistics/National Centre for Language Teaching and Research/Centre for Language in Social Life, Macquarie University

Lea, M and Stierer, B (2000) *Student Writing in Higher Education*, Society for Research into Higher Education and Open University Press, Buckingham

Leki, I (1992) *Understanding ESL Writers. A guide for teachers*, Boynton-Cook, Portsmouth

Maher, J (1986) English for medical purposes, *Language Teaching*, **19**, pp 112–45

Mauch, J and Birch, J (1993) *Guide to the Successful Thesis and Dissertation: A handbook for students and faculty*, Marcel Dekker, New York

Maxwell, M (2000) Foreword, in *Handbook of College Reading and Study Strategy Research*, ed R Flippo and D Caverly, Lawrence Erlbaum, Mahwah, NJ

McGrath, D and Townsend, B (1996) Strengthening the preparedness of at risk students, in *Handbook of the Undergraduate Curriculum*, eds J Gaff and J Ratcliff, Jossey-Bass, San Francisco

McInnes, C and James, R (1995) *First Year on Campus*, Australian Government Publishing Service, Canberra

McLean, P, Surtie, F, Elphinstone, L and Devlin, M (1995) Models of learning support in Victorian universities: issues and implications, *Higher Education Research and Development*, **14** (1)

Murphy, D, Walker, R and Webb, G (eds) (2001) *Online Learning and Teaching with Technology: Case Studies, Experience and Profile*, Kogan Page, London

Pascarella, E and Terenzini, P (1983) Predicting voluntary freshmen year persistence/withdrawal behaviour in a residential university: a path analytic validation of Tinto's model, *Journal of Educational Psychology*, **75** (2), pp 215–26

Pugh, S, Pawan, F and Antommarchi, C (2000) Academic literacy and the new college learner, in *Handbook of College Reading and Study Strategy Research*, eds R Flippo and D Caverly, Lawrence Erlbaum, Mahwah, NJ

Riley, A (1991) *English for Law*, Macmillan, Leicester

Rosenblatt, L (1994) The transactional theory of reading and writing, in *Theoretical Models and Processes of Reading*, eds R Ruddel, M Ruddel and H Singer, International Reading Association, Delaware

Ryan, Y and Zuber-Skerritt, O (1999) *Supervising Postgraduates from Non-English-Speaking Backgrounds*, Open University Press, Buckingham

Schwartz, P, Mennin, S and Webb, G (eds) (2001) *Problem Based Learning. Case Studies, Experience and Practice*, Kogan Page, London

Schwartz, P and Webb, G (1993) *Case Studies on Teaching in Higher Education*, Kogan Page, London

Schwartz, P and Webb, G (2002) *Assessment, Case Studies and Practice from Higher Education*, Kogan Page, London

Stahl, N and King, J (2000) A history of college reading, in *A Handbook of College Reading and Study Strategy Research*, ed R Flippo and D Caverly, Lawrence Erlbaum, Mahwah, NJ

Swales, J (1990) *Genre Analysis,* Cambridge University Press, Cambridge

Swales, J and Feak, C (1994) *Academic Writing for Graduate Students,* University of Michigan Press, Michigan

Tinto, V (1975) Dropout from higher education: a theoretical synthesis of recent research, *Review of Educational Research*, **45** (1), pp 89–125

Trimble, L (1990) *English for Science and Technology,* Cambridge University Press, Cambridge

Webb, J (2001) Using the web to explore issues related to the first year experience, *Higher Education Research and Development*, **20** (2), pp 225–36

RELATING TO STUDENTS

CHAPTER 1

Mentoring rosie

Case reporter: Martha Bean

Issues raised

This case study raises issues of cultural diversity within a university faculty–student mentoring programme, including the effectiveness of mentoring for mentees from different cultural, linguistic, and socio-economic backgrounds.

Background

The events in the case study occurred at San José State University, a public university that is part of the California State University system USA. The San José State campus serves approximately 27,000 students, most of whom live off campus, and is located in the South Bay area of California, also known as Silicon Valley, about an hour south-east of San Francisco.

PART 1

Rocío, or Rosie, Ramirez was a young woman of Mexican-American descent. She had graduated from high school and decided to apply to the local four-year university in San José, where she lived. This was a momentous decision. Rosie's parents had migrated from Mexico and speak little English. As Rosie's mother said to her, 'I only went to middle school and your father only went through fifth grade. Neither of us know much about going to university or going to college.' Rosie's mother let her know how proud they were that she wanted to go to college. But both Rosie and her parents knew that her parents were struggling with a mortgage and low wages. They couldn't possibly co-sign a loan for Rosie's tuition. And as her parents had been so busy with work and keeping things going, they had neither been monitoring her courses in high school nor exploring future university options with her. And even if they had the time, Rosie knew that they did not have the knowledge or experience to be able to help her.

Rosie knew that she was at a distinct disadvantage compared to her classmates from more middle class, non-immigrant families, who saw going to college as a natural next step. Their only concern was which college they would attend. But Rosie learnt from her high school classmates that a degree in criminal justice would enable her to join the police force and that she would have to attend a four-year university. She had received little guidance counselling from school on her ambition, but she knew that living in California was an advantage. There is a network of public two-year community colleges, as well as two parallel university systems: the prestigious University of California (UC) system and the more working class oriented California State University (CSU) system.

Rosie noticed that her classmates were talking about going to four-year schools, so she decided to visit the local CSU in search of application materials. 'This is so different from high school,' she thought as she reached the college campus in her search of information. She began to feel anxious. Who would she turn to for help when she had problems? Her parents would not be able to help her; they had never been to college themselves. She knew that this was a college, but how did it relate to the university? Who could help her when she had problems with her studies? Where would she go if she was ill? How would she use the college library? Rose did not know it yet, but there were many other things that she would have to learn, such as choosing the optimal slate of courses for her intended major, the greatly increased academic load in terms of reading and writing, and dealing with unfamiliar professors in large classes and with students of all ages.

Finally, Rosie applied to San José State University (SJSU), a campus that, as a result of recent waves of immigration, was very culturally diverse. She had already found out that there were students from Latino, Vietnamese, Chinese, and Filipino language and cultural backgrounds. Fortunately for Rosie, the SJSU realized that its many minority students needed significant help in order to succeed.

The spring before she actually started attending the university, among her admissions materials Rosie caught sight of a flier for the Faculty Mentor Program, a programme designed specifically to help entering students. She signed up for the programme.

What do you think Rosie's major difficulties will be?
How do you think the mentor programme will help Rosie?

PART 2

August was fast approaching, and Rosie had been accepted at San José State University. Her parents were proud of their youngest daughter's accomplishments, but anxious about the unknown challenges she would face, especially as she adjusted to her freshman year. A few weeks into July, a paper arrived from the Faculty Mentor Program. It told her the name of the SJSU faculty member who was to be her mentor during her freshman year.

The paper went out of Rosie's mind as she struggled to survive her first two weeks of classes: getting to school on time, finding parking in the crowded environs of the university, and using the campus map to locate her first classes. The workload seemed enormous compared with high school, and her college textbooks seemed outrageously expensive, but Rosie was determined.

During week three, the phone rang at her home during the evening. It was me calling. 'Hi, my name is Dr Martha Bean and I am your faculty mentor. It is my job to help you with any questions or difficulties that you might have.'

Rosie was one of the first mentees I worked with in the Faculty Mentor Program. I was concerned about the age gap (I was in my early fifties and Rosie in her late teens), but felt very comfortable with Rosie's Mexican-American heritage. Years earlier, I had worked in Central America and South America and become familiar with the Spanish language and the core values among Latino cultures, mostly a great love of family and of the church.

I invited Rosie to join me for a meal at the University Room, a faculty dining room in which students are also welcome. When we met, Rosie was shy and quiet. This concerned me, because I knew that in order to survive well at the university, students needed to be proactive and, at times, outspoken. I was also concerned about Rosie's academic programme. Some universities block registration until a student has seen an adviser, but not SJSU. Therefore, many students sign up for a schedule of classes that is not in their best interest. I began our first conversation with a discussion of backgrounds and interests and Rosie's academic and career goals. I did not know anything about her intended major, administrative justice (AJ), but I did know that she would benefit more from seeing an adviser in AJ rather than a general adviser in Admissions and Records.

Rosie told me that she was uncertain about her college experience; she was not sure that her courses were the best for her AJ major. I helped her locate the office of the AJ department on campus. In fact, I called a personal contact in that department and asked him about advising procedures. He was most encouraging and suggested that Rosie go to the departmental office. Rosie was nervous about what to say in this setting, so we practised what she might say to the departmental secretary to achieve her goal of getting an AJ adviser.

Over bi-monthly breakfast or lunch meetings, Rosie told me that she was concerned about her academic writing. She did not understand the campus milestones such as the Writing Skills Test (at the end of a student's sophomore year or the beginning of a student's junior year), and even graduation requirements: 120 units in all. I explained to her the next steps at the sophomore-level Writing Skills Test and advised her to aim for at least a B or 3.0 grade point average in succeeding semesters, especially in her last two years of study, if she wanted to do graduate work.

But Rosie had more immediate concerns. Her low score on the English Placement Test taken over the summer (an admissions requirement) meant that she was in a remedial Acadmic English class. She had to do a lot of writing. She also had to pass a final exam of a timed essay to go on to the required English 1A class. I could sense Rosie's stress when she told me that, unlike high school, many of her courses required extensive writing assignments. Although her high school teachers had praised Rosie's writing, her papers were now coming back with many red marks and negative comments. This was distressing Rosie; she realized that a much higher quality of writing was expected in her academic work, and also in her professional work after graduation. Would Rosie be able to cope with the writing demands of her study, and would I be equipped to support her in this process?

If you were the mentor in this situation, what would you do?
What do you think actually happened?

PART 3

I could help Rosie a little in her maths and AJ courses, but writing was where I had special expertise. So I referred Rosie to a writing centre on campus, the Intensive Learning Experience, which provides direct assistance with grammatical points and suggestions on academic writing style, as well as planning and getting started on writing assignments. With this extra help, Rosie became more confident and at ease in her course assignments. They helped her analyse her task so that she was clear on the focus she should take in her written piece, and about structuring particular pieces of writing, such as reports and essays. Another area where they helped her a lot was with the more formal type of language used in academic writing. Gradually, Rosie came to understand that the way she spoke at home was different from what was expected in her writing. At first, Rosie was upset about this, thinking that the way her family spoke was in some ways inferior, and she struggled to retain her developing confidence as she addressed this point. But I made a point of explaining to Rosie that the way she spoke at home to her family was not wrong. Using examples, I helped her to see that we use language in different ways for different purposes. For example, when we were speaking in our mentoring sessions, the words we used were sometimes quite different from those we would use if we were writing. Gradually, Rosie came to understand that the ways she was used to doing things were just different. The result was that, rather than completely wiping her home style of language from her repertoire, Rosie soon learnt to use language appropriate for particular situations. She became proud of her ability to use language in different ways for particular purposes.

Rosie and I began to communicate much more easily following this development. It seemed that we understood each other and Rosie was able to confide in me. In fact, a family situation had been causing her great distress. Although it was in an area beyond my role and expertise as a faculty mentor, I had access to information about campus and community resources and I could direct Rosie to places for assistance. I knew that Rosie was feeling anxious, so I directed her to Counseling Services on campus, where there were counsellors who were highly sensitive to the culturally diverse population. As Rosie was unaware of other resources available to the student body, I provided her with information about the Student Health Center, the Disability Resource Center, the Career Center, the Chicano Resource Center, and the Student Life Center. I was pleased when Rosie inquired about the sororities and fraternities on campus; she realized that she needed friends as part of establishing a balance between her studies, her part-time job, and personal life.

What do you feel are the most important ways in which faculty mentors can help students such as Rosie?
What other ways could the faculty mentor have helped Rosie?
How might a mentoring programme work in your own situation?

CASE REPORTER'S DISCUSSION

A seminal aspect of my relationship with Rosie was that we were able to establish a successful relationship early on. Both she and I kept in contact and kept our mentoring appointments. Feedback from faculty mentors and mentees suggests that as many as one-third of mentoring relationships never 'get off the ground'. The faculty mentor is unable to establish initial contact because phone calls are not returned or appointments are not kept. Although the Faculty Mentor Program has not formally investigated why this might be so, experienced mentors guess that in some cases, students who sign up for the mentor programme grasp neither the time commitment required in terms of talking or meeting with the mentor, nor the very real advantages that the programme offers long term.

Areas in which the mentor programme is able to offer little help are problems like family health crises (mental or physical) or serious financial problems. When students fail to return to the university for such reasons, faculty mentors are powerless to offer assistance, beyond providing information on sources of possible assistance on campus or in the community. Rosie and I were fortunate that her family crisis did not derail her college education. However, if Rosie had had to leave the university for a semester, I could have told her how to make a 'returning student' application. This would have allowed her to return to the university after an unplanned leave of one semester rather than having to apply all over again. Likewise, if Rosie had to drop a class after the drop period, I could show her how to do a retroactive drop that would give her a 'W' or 'withdraw' on her transcript. This is far less damaging than the 'F' that students get who fail to do an administrative drop on time or retroactively.

One area in which Rosie received little or no assistance from me was in her major. I knew little about the subject area of administrative justice, and even less about conferences and career opportunities that might be available to AJ majors. I was able neither to be a successful AJ role model for Rosie nor to share with her career tips or suggestions that might have made her adjustment to her chosen field a smoother affair. As a result of this disadvantage, at least one college of SJSU, the College of Humanities and the Arts, has requested that incoming students who have declared a major in one of the eight departments of the college be assigned faculty mentors from those departments. In humanities and in the arts particularly, it turns out that a faculty mentor in theatre, dance or music can mentor a student in these areas far more effectively than a faculty member from engineering or business. At SJSU, however, the practice of matching mentors and mentees on the basis of major soon breaks down. Most of the entering students, declare a major in business or engineering while most of the mentors are from other areas of the university.

Two areas that did seem to work well for us were ethnicity and gender. I generally request Latino students because of my own familiarity with Latino culture. This 'match' seems to work well for me and for my mentees. Because of my interest in things Latino, I am aware of the area's demographics and of the socio-economic situation of many Latino families. Another helpful attribute was my ability to speak Spanish. Sometimes initial mentee contact calls fail because of language; the faculty mentor is simply unable to communicate with a family member who answers the phone because of language differences. For Rosie and me, this was not a problem. I was soon on a 'chatting' basis with her family and if Rosie's mother answered the phone, we could communicate as easily in Spanish as in English.

Regarding gender, it was perhaps no small benefit to Rosie that I am a female in a profession that has traditionally been male-dominated (the professoriate). Likewise, the many professions within administrative justice, police work and so on, have traditionally been male-dominated. As Rosie's mother had stayed at home raising her family for much of her life, it was helpful for

Rosie to be mentored by a professional woman. In fact, at one point Rosie was having difficulty with a part-time employer. I was able to give her advice on how to be professionally assertive and how to set appropriate boundaries in the workplace. Regarding gender and ethnicity, both the mentor application form and the mentee application form ask applicants if they have any ethnicity or gender preferences, and the matching process honours such preferences as much as possible.

Another area of success in Rosie's and my mentoring relationship was what I call the 'doing school' factor. While my value as an AJ mentor was low, I was more helpful in areas such as managing time, developing learning and study strategies, making friends at school, choosing courses wisely, dealing with institutional bureaucracy, and so on. These are survival strategies which people in academe hone to a fine art. Likewise, another benefit to the mentee is that the faculty mentor has many personal contacts among faculty and staff. When Rosie ran into family problems, I was able to contact Counseling Services people I knew personally. When Rosie experienced difficulty in getting money from one of her grants, I was able to call the Assistant Director of Financial Aid personally and got through much faster than Rosie would have been able to. In this sense, mentoring amounts to 'having a friend in your corner', something like a big brother or a big sister as well as someone who knows the rest of the family well.

It would be remiss to conclude without mentioning the many benefits to faculty members as well. Faculty mentors at San José State are considered volunteers, but do receive a small stipend of $150 per academic year per mentee. Remuneration is provided in the form of reimbursement for expenses rather than cash, and many mentors use their stipends in ways that will assist their mentees, for example, paying for mentees' meals or books or conference travel. Other mentors use their stipends to offset their own academic expenses, which might be reimbursement for books or travel.

Most mentors, however, report that benefits to them personally far outweigh any remuneration. Times have changed substantially since most faculty members were students themselves. Working one on one with students who are not in their classes, that is, not under their authority or beholden to them for grades, gives faculty mentors the chance to get a real-life glimpse of the challenges being faced by today's students. Mentoring Rosie provided this glimpse for me. Among other benefits, it allowed me to look at SJSU life through the eyes of a shy student who was the first in her family to attend college and whose parents spoke little English. These understandings gave me new insight into and empathy for my own students and led me to give, not easier tasks and assignments in my classes, but more accessible and appropriate tasks and assignments. I would like to credit Rosie as an important part of my decision to do more small group work in classes, to do more one-on-one work with students during office hours, to break up major writing assignments into smaller, more manageable parts, and to seek student feedback in many and varied ways throughout the semester rather than waiting for the final evaluations. These decisions have yielded markedly improved performance on the part of my students.

It appears that the Faculty Mentor Program does bring tangible positive outcomes to students like Rosie as well. Tracking of students in the Faculty Mentor Program has shown that they have a slightly higher grade point average than do students not in the programme, complete a slightly higher number of units per semester, and have a markedly increased rate of retention: 25 per cent over the norm for the university as a whole. Rosie's experience bears out these statistics.

Rosie and I both opted to continue the mentoring relationship after her freshman year for the remaining three years of her college education. The graduation party at Rosie's home given by her proud parents was one of the happiest events that we shared along her journey. Rosie has since been gain-fully and successfully employed in several AJ-related posts since her graduation. She has also married and, together with her husband, purchased their first home and had their first child. Despite her rather humble beginnings, she is realizing the so-called American dream and, perhaps not coincidentally, fulfilling the mission of San José State University, which is to educate its graduates to serve the community well through the professions. For students like Rosie, participating in the Faculty Mentor Program is like taking out insurance on the dream and constitutes one more way of improving one's chances of success, especially at the university. In Rosie's case, it seems to have worked.

CHAPTER 2

THE HEART AND THE MACHINE

Case reporter: Janet Robbins

Issues raised

The main issue in this case is how best to assist a student whose problems in learning to use computers are largely based on attitude. The complex nature of the relationship between academic adviser and academic staff, and the boundaries of the academic adviser's role, are also raised.

Background

This incident took place at an Australian institute of creative arts in the late 1990s. It concerned a full fee-paying mature aged female student enrolled in a course involving computer assisted graphic design.

PART 1

Helen had been working as an academic skills adviser for three years. Previously, she had been an academic with some 20 years' university teaching experience in her own discipline. She was known as a skilled and patient teacher who usually achieved friendly relationships with students. She had also had experience for five years outside the university, designing educational multimedia. In this job she had had some experience with computer-based graphics applications.

The academic learning centre where Helen worked was very student centred and individual consultations were a key service. Because of the sensitivity of university politics in an age of budget cuts, the centre was also careful to maintain good relations with academic staff. Helen had learnt a number of things during her years at the centre, including dressing more casually than when she had worked as an academic, deliberately minimizing the social distance between herself and the student. She knew that she had only a few seconds in which to establish rapport, and first impressions counted.

Marina was a new student who came to see Helen one day. As per her usual practice, Helen greeted Marina warmly, and invited her to sit in a comfortable chair close to the corner of Helen's desk (another attempt to create a relaxed and friendly environment where hopes and fears could be openly discussed). Helen asked Marina which course she was enrolled in, and other basic information for the record card. Then she quietly asked her how she could help.

The following tangled situation emerged. Marina, a mature aged student from another English-speaking country, explained to Helen that she had enrolled in a full fee-paying Masters course focusing on the use of information technology (IT) in the creative arts. She was already a graduate in visual arts at the time of her enrolment, and had travelled and worked as a successful artist for many years before she decided to broaden her skills to include new media. She entered the Masters course after completing a short course using 'Paintworks' in her home country. However, Marina openly acknowledged that she 'did not understand the course very well'.

Marina explained to Helen that when she applied for the Masters course before she arrived in Australia, she had pointed out in initial discussions with the staff that she did not think she had a strong background in the use of computers. However, the course convenor reassured her that she would be able to manage. (It seems that the staff in the creative arts department were intent on recruiting more students.) It was now more than half-way through the semester, and Marina was in great distress. She said that she was not coping at all with the unit on Paintworks.

Marina showed Helen some of her art and Helen was very impressed. 'These illustrations are truly beautiful, Marina. You must be a very skilled artist to be able to produce these!' she commented. Somewhat cheered, Marina explained, 'My project is to make an electronic book. I have some wonderful poems here that I want to integrate with some of my paintings.' 'Well, although I only know a little about Paintworks, I would not think that would be too hard. It's a very powerful application', responded Helen. Privately, Helen thought that, since Marina's project was not very difficult, and she clearly had considerable skill in another area, her problems might not be the usual ones of dealing with a difficult subject area.

'But I'm finding the course very confusing,' wailed Marina. 'I feel quite overwhelmed now. It goes at such a pace. Even though I go in to the computer lab to practise in my own time, I can't keep up with all the new things he's teaching us. I don't think I can do it! He assumes so much knowledge about computers, even though I *told* them I didn't have much background before I came here!'

'Well, can you ask for help? Or ask him to slow down?' asked Helen.

'I *do* ask! But he's become very angry with me. I think he knows I'm going to fail and he's given up trying to help me. He just brushes me off now when I ask a question. Says he can't spend all his time helping me. He even told me in front of the class last week that I was stupid.' Marina was crying now. 'I'm so nervous now in class, that I just make more mistakes – I do silly things, like closing windows without saving. And then he makes more sarcastic comments. I can't sleep thinking about it. I was away sick last week, I'd got so run down – I am still sick now – but missing class made it even worse when I came back. I feel really depressed about it.'

'Hmm,' said Helen, thinking fast. 'Are there any other students who might help you? Are you friends with anyone in the class?'

Marina replied despairingly, 'I haven't had time to get to know anyone much. I only got here two days before the course started and we've been flat out from the beginning. Besides, they're all too busy on their own stuff. Everyone's really pushing to get their projects finished. The lab technician helps me a bit. He's friendly and tries to be nice, but he's too busy fixing computers and dealing with the whole class and it's not his job.'

Becoming desperate for inspiration as the situation became gloomier and gloomier, Helen then suggested that perhaps there were other people who could tutor Marina in the application. 'That would cost money, though,' explained Helen.

Marina responded that she had thought of that, but didn't have any money to spare. 'I'm living on the poverty line as it is,' said Marina.

Helen then sought to place Marina's problems into a wider context and inquired how her other units were going. But she sensed from Marina's body language that there was yet more to this tale of woe.

Marina heaved a big sigh and looked even more glum. 'My teacher and class mates criticized my paintings the other day in my studio unit. They said I was too old fashioned in my approach. Not *avant garde* enough. I was really crushed. I've always had really good feedback on my work before this.' She started to cry again. 'I think I should drop the Paintworks unit, even though it is the one I particularly came here to do. I've even thought about withdrawing from the whole course and going home.'

Helen glanced quickly at the calendar. 'Um, it's too late to get a refund on any fees, Marina,' she said very gently, 'and you'll get recorded as a fail in any units you withdraw from now. It is better to stay in there and let's see what we can do to help.'

What do you think are the main factors contributing to Marina's problems?
What should Helen do?
What do you think Helen will do?

PART 2

Helen considered whether she should contact the teacher and discuss the situation with him. She hesitated to do this, because if, as seemed quite possible, he resented her intervention, it could have repercussions for Marina. Also, she could see that it would not be easy to discuss the problem in general terms. As soon as she described the situation to the teacher, Marina would immediately be identifiable, so this was probably not a good option. She would need Marina's permission to break the confidentiality of the consultation in any case, so she raised the prospect to see how Marina felt.

'Would you like me to ring him and discuss the issue with him?' she asked tentatively.

'No, definitely not!' Marina responded promptly. 'It would only make things much worse.'

Helen nodded. Marina's response confirmed her own judgement, and she was relieved not to have a potentially unpleasant confrontation to deal with. Through her sympathetic listening and acceptance, Helen had now established good rapport with Marina, so she felt comfortable in suggesting to Marina that she consult the Counselling and Health Services for help with her anxiety, depression, insomnia and her lingering illness. Helen also considered whether, since this was largely a problem of attitude rather than cognitive learning, referring Marina to Counselling would be enough to solve the problem. Helen felt that the crux of the problem lay in the interaction between Marina's attitude and the cognitive task of learning to use the computer, and that consequently she could also usefully contribute to its resolution.

To this end, Helen shared her own experiences of falling in her ice-skating lessons, as a way of showing how many of us internalize failure to mean that we cannot learn something, rather than accepting mistakes as a natural and inevitable part of learning.

To address the computer anxiety, Helen took Marina over to her own computer, and revised some basic file management procedures with her. Then Helen opened up four applications at once and deliberately crashed her computer, joking that, 'I always crash at least three times a day, because I expect computers to be able to do anything I want them to. But see, as long as you've saved often (every few minutes if you are dealing with big graphics files), and backed up regularly, it doesn't matter if you crash. And remember, whatever goes wrong, it's never your fault, it's always the fault of the computer or the software manufacturer. I always swear at my computer. The computer doesn't care, but swearing makes me feel less frustrated.'

Marina stared at her for a minute, then suddenly laughed uproariously as she saw the contrast to her own way of blaming herself whenever anything went wrong. Helen then made Marina sit down and explore a simple paint program in whatever way she wanted to, just having fun, but remembering to save and back-up frequently. In this way, Helen normalized Marina's experiences with the computer. In the process, Helen essentially reframed the learning task from an impossible chore to a game, where mistakes were expected and even greeted with laughter. By the end of that session, Marina still felt inclined to drop the unit rather than continue to deal with the teacher's condescending behaviour, but on the other hand she still wanted to continue to learn Paintworks, and now believed that she could do it.

Next, Helen met Marina after hours at the computer lab. They sat together and shared their knowledge about Paintworks and played with the application, with Helen giving occasional reminders about saving or backing-up. After a short period of mutual giggling, experimentation and joking, Marina took over and began to enjoy herself, exploring different tools and options, somewhat to the bemusement of the lab technician. It quickly became apparent that she actually knew quite a lot and the two-hour session was completed with her confidence at least partly restored. Marina did not come back to see Helen, who heard later that Marina had indeed withdrawn from the Paintworks unit, but had persisted with the studio unit and was doing well.

Marina's problems were alleviated through learning how to approach her mistakes constructively. However, Helen made no attempt to contact the teacher directly, even after she discovered that Marina had withdrawn from the unit. She avoided confronting him. As a consequence of many students failing and many complaints about his behaviour, the teacher's contract was not renewed. This made Helen wonder whether she should in fact have found a way of tactfully giving him some feedback, even though technically this was not her primary responsibility, and might itself have prejudiced his attitude toward the centre.

CASE REPORTER'S DISCUSSION

As Helen reviewed her diagnosis of the problems, and her options for helping Marina, several key points came to mind. Clearly, Marina was not adjusting at all to education in Australia. She had made few friends, and apart from Helen as the academic skills adviser, had little in the way of learning support around her. Perhaps this had intensified Marina's homesickness. But Marina's description of her background, given early in the consultation, suggested she was an independent single woman, who had travelled widely and usually had little contact with her family. Still, the fact that she had few friends in Australia might certainly be a part of the problem.

Could Marina in fact be unable to learn to use the computer application? Although this was apparently the teacher's conclusion, it did not seem to fit with the fact that, despite her own account of 'not understanding' the earlier Paintworks course, she had initially believed that she *could* learn the application. Also, the task she had chosen should be within reach of most people. And it did not fit with her previous successes. There must be more to Marina's predicament.

In the end, Helen's analysis was that after her negative experiences with the teacher, Marina had decided that she could not learn in this situation. Like other mature aged women students with whom Helen had worked, Marina may have been nervous about returning to study and disappointed that she had not quickly found a supportive relationship with her teacher. She had then transferred her negative feelings about the teacher to both the subject matter and her own ability to learn it. As a result, she had lost most of her confidence. Her situation was exacerbated by her general anxiety about using computers, the critical response to her work in her studio course, and by the fact that she had no support network at the institute.

This situation leads to the issue of the extent of the academic skill adviser's responsibility in dealing with emotional or attitudinal problems. Tertiary study deals with difficult concepts and skills and is by its very nature challenging, so that even very good students experience stress. Many of the students who come for academic help are in some degree of emotional distress, although only a proportion will reveal this overtly. Serious emotional or mental health issues are beyond the skills of most advisers, and any attempt to deal with them could have serious consequences (such as suicide or litigation). So it is important to be able to recognize and refer such serious problems to Counselling, if necessary accompanying a student in crisis to the Counselling Centre. However, even though advisers routinely refer emotionally vulnerable students to Counselling, there is no guarantee that students will attend even when an adviser makes the appointment for them. Also, lack of immediate action on emotional issues may leave the student too upset to benefit much from the academic advice on the study issues that are causing or compounding the upset. Advisers thus need some basic 'first aid' skills in dealing with upset students on the spot.

The kind of emotional first aid that is useful includes careful and sympathetic listening, while gently exploring the academic problems and options, never blaming the student for the situation, but treating the problem as just a part of the learning experience. Judging or moralizing about what the student should have done only increases the student's distress and self-blame and can paralyse him or her. Instead, pointing out that even failing a whole semester's units is not the end of the world, or sharing one's own failures, can help create a little calm emotional space for prioritizing, planning and deciding on effective strategies.

Marina had no confidence in working on the computer and interpreted errors as solely due to her poor performance. Students can experience learning to use a computer as a series of disconnected procedures requiring rote learning rather than understanding. Marina might have lacked a conceptual framework of how computers work, so she could not make sensible guesses as to how to do things, but only repeat a trial and error approach. Further, Helen believed that many women had been encultured into a timid approach to computers. They often seemed afraid of 'breaking the computer', or at least destroying hours of work with their mistakes. In contrast, although male students typically also learnt IT tasks by experimentation, their attempts tended to be more systematic. Moreover, they rarely took failures to signify a lack of personal ability, as women seemed to. Hence, Helen intuitively felt that it was important to give women students such as Marina some concept of how computers worked, reassure them that they were unlikely to damage the actual computer, and teach them sound back-up and other IT 'insurance' practices early, so as to lower their anxiety levels and free them to experiment.

Helen also realized that to the academic, in a class of mostly younger and more computer literate students, Marina may have appeared both overly dependent and a poor student. It might also have been that the teacher was young and inexperienced, although in Helen's mind this did not excuse the teacher's unsympathetic behaviour.

Nevertheless, Helen was faced with a dilemma, beyond that of the best way to help the student. Centre policy was always to deal very tactfully with academic staff, and certainly to never try to do their job by teaching a subject area. Students in need of content help should be referred back to the academic concerned. But Helen guessed that this would be unlikely to work in this case. It seemed that Marina's relationship with the teacher concerned was so bad that she would be unlikely to take up such a suggestion, or if she did, that his response might be negative, worsening the situation.

Working with staff is another area where advisers may be challenged to step outside their job description. In some centres, helping staff with teaching or curriculum problems may be a well accepted part of their role. However, in Helen's institution, the teaching staff were assisted in respect to teaching by a different centre. This had some advantages in terms of staff and students in dispute not meeting in the waiting room, or advisers having divided loyalties in trying to deal with both sides. Its disadvantage was that academic staff could not officially get advice from those with experience of the problems from the students' side. Informally, however, some staff did seek advice from advisers they knew, and advisers did sometimes ring academics to say things like, 'Look, we are seeing a lot of students who don't know what to do in this assignment, because it is a new genre for them. It might be worth taking five minutes in class to explain it to everyone.'

The teacher in Marina's case sounded very unhelpful, but perhaps this was because he was also struggling. That was why Helen felt rather guilty that she had not contacted him to say, even if it was not quite the truth, 'I've seen some of your students who are finding the pace in class too fast. They need more help. Is there any way you could provide some handouts, for instance, so that students could work through them in their own time? Or perhaps you could organize the students into groups to work through some learning exercises before they go off to work on their projects? That way they could help each other.'

Perhaps if Helen had contacted him and tactfully made such suggestions out of her own teaching experience, he might have been able to improve his teaching and both he and all of the students would have benefited.

Because he was male, this teacher might also have felt unable to deal with this student's need for encouragement and reassurance. Female students may find the university experience more alienating than men do, particularly in situations like Honours or postgraduate studies where they are expected to work closely with one (usually male) supervisor. Mature aged female students, in particular, often have very high standards for themselves, and may simultaneously be anxious and diffident in their approach, as Marina was. They may also be more sensitive than male students or teachers to the nuances of non-verbal communication or frequency of contact. This can lead to their misinterpreting the apparent coldness or impatience of an overworked academic as a comment on their failure as a student. It is difficult for an adviser to know what is really going on in such situations. Sometimes the student needs to be reminded that academics often have no special training in relating to people, and thus the student should not take the academic's responses personally, but seek encouragement and emotional support from counsellors, advisers and friends. However, sometimes there is a case of real neglect, poor communication or outright discrimination and hostility which requires very careful intervention and negotiation, and possibly a change of unit or supervisor to rectify.

Helen also saw that Marina urgently needed very practical hands-on help, bordering on content instruction. Helen knew a little about the application, and quite a lot about computers. If Marina needed help that badly, Helen might be able to give it. Helen's instinct as a teacher was that she needed to model some robust learning strategies in Paintworks for Marina to gain confidence and break through her paralysing anxieties. But where and how could she give this hands-on help? Helen did not have Paintworks on her computer, so she could not explore its use with Marina in privacy. It was not on any university computers that could be accessed, except in the dedicated electronic media laboratory belonging to the course, which was in almost constant use, 24 hours a day, by classes or students working on their projects. And if they went there, the danger was that the teacher might ask questions, potentially involving the academic skills centre in an unpleasant exchange and possibly damaging its reputation.

It is true that, over time, most advisers end up with a broad (and perhaps superficial) knowledge of the academic disciplines with which they work. Such knowledge may be useful in explaining to a student why an answer to a question received a low mark, by mentioning some of the content that *could* have been included, and so illustrating the level of detail needed. Knowledge implicit in an essay draft may need to be made explicit for students to recognize that they have left out a crucial step in an argument. The danger with this use of content is that advisers are not experts, and may mislead students, who then could incorporate misinformation into assignments. This has repercussions for the centre's reputation with both students and academics. Often the same pedagogical aims can be achieved by questioning, rather than giving information directly. However, even asking useful questions presupposes some knowledge and imagination.

These are complex issues which may require consultation and policy development with other academic skills advisers. Advisers need to be clear as to how best to assist students in the context of their particular institute or university. It is for the benefit of students such as Marina, academic staff, academic skills advisers like Helen and the institution overall that discussion such as this takes place.

CHAPTER 3

DOING IT HARD

Case reporter: Ormond Simpson

Issues raised

The main issue raised in this case is how teachers' emotions and values can be critically exposed when working with students of whose behaviour they disapprove.

Background

This case occurred at the Open University in the UK. It concerns the tuition that was provided on site for prison inmates. I was the Open University link for the Education Department of a high security prison. The students were Gary and Ron, both serving life sentences for serious crimes.

PART 1

'Scuse me, Sir!' the gatekeeper's bellow echoed down the street after me. I stopped short, feeling exactly like a six-year-old who'd just nicked a sweet from the newsagent's. Actually, I had just spent a couple of hours feeling like that: I had been visiting a prison for the first time and the experience of being shepherded through a dozen doors, unlocked and locked behind me again and again, had reduced me to an infantile state.

Finally, I had been allowed out of the old prison gate into the street and was moving away as fast as dignity allowed. Then came the shout: and very slowly I made my way back. What archaic Home Office regulation had I transgressed? What sentence would I receive? 'You're from the Open University, sir?' the gatekeeper said heavily. I confessed to this usually minor crime. He produced a newspaper. 'Can you work out the answer to five across?' he said. It was a notorious tabloid and fortunately it was not too difficult to maintain the university's academic credibility.

I guess that almost anyone who has visited prison has felt that infantile state and the curious unreality that pervades prison contacts. Here I am discussing quantum mechanics with an inmate in as everyday a manner as discussing quantum mechanics ever gets. But he is in the middle of a 15-year sentence and I cannot help wondering what he did in some terrifying moment six or seven years ago. Of course I do not ask – and generally they do not tell me, although I do remember sitting across from one particularly well built, would-be social scientist with a fearsome scar running across his cheek and lip. 'Actually, Ormond,' he confided, leaning across to me, 'I'm in here for financial impropriety.' 'Armed robbery,' said the Education Officer as we left.

But there are incongruities in prison all the time. I have often talked with students about 'assessment stress': the anxiety many of them feel when submitting and subsequently getting back a marked assignment. That was put into context for me by the inmate who had just started his first course. 'Getting that first assignment back was the most stressful point of my whole life,' he confided to me. 'In his previous career he was pursued through the streets of London by armed police,' said the Education Officer as we left, 'so he must know a bit about stress.'

Working with students in prison is surreal, stressful, demanding on feelings and moral judgements. Sometimes it is funny – almost gallows humour. And occasionally it is deeply worthwhile.

Gary was in for life. Unfortunately I knew about his crime, as it had been committed locally. He had abducted a three-year-old girl, raped her, murdered her and thrown the body into a river. It still makes me feel sick as I relate the crime.

So how was I to respond when I received a note from the prison to say that Gary had applied to do a course at my institution? The prison Education Department has a clear policy: where an inmate is capable of progressing studies at university level and is not a danger to the tutor or other inmates, then the application must be put forward. There was also another, less obvious reason. Gary was clearly on the brink of insanity. Rotting in jail with nothing to do was quite likely to push him over the brink, and then he would be much more of a problem. Study, the prison staff reason, is likely to be both occupational and mental therapy – and it might make him easier to manage.

But I had the last say. I could have refused, saving public money on his fees. I could also have saved myself the distasteful task of asking a tutor to visit him. Of course I would not have told the tutor of Gary's crime, but it would not have made any difference: Gary would have told them at some point. He is not supposed to, but in the context of a one to one tutorial it is very difficult to stop him. Perhaps he gets a creepy kind of satisfaction from relating his story.

So the application form was on my desk. I could pass it to the Enrolments Section for processing. Or I could screw it up and throw it away and no one would blame me. As an educator, I had ordinary liberal values and a wish to help the disadvantaged members of society. But I also felt an overwhelming repugnance towards Gary's crime and – frankly – to Gary himself. This was intensified by the course that he had chosen. Gary, the paedophile and child killer, wanted to take child psychology. What was his motive? I could not ignore the thought racing through my mind that I could actually be assisting him to become a cleverer paedophile. So my dilemma was whether I should pass on the application, or screw it up.

Ron's was another case that had etched itself in my brain. He had been inside prison for about nine years when I met him. I never asked why he was there, but you do not get a long sentence in one of Britain's most notorious top-security prisons for double-parking your truck. And that is what he had been in his previous life: a lorry driver. It still showed in his build, which was like a road-train. He would have made a good bouncer.

Somewhere in those nine years the Education Department had spotted a talent in Ron. He had no previous qualifications, but had started doing some school maths courses and had blossomed. When I met him he was near to completing his degree, having taken some of the toughest courses the university has to offer: 'Number Theory and Mathematical Logic', 'The Lebesgue Integral', 'Differential Geometry'. I was a pre-transistor physicist and I recognized the content but could not begin to understand it.

But Ron had discovered another talent too: for teaching. Under his tutelage a number of other inmates were studying. Ron had immense patience and gentleness, and perhaps it was partly due to him that the institution often had the best course results of any prison in the UK.

Last year he graduated. He narrowly missed a First Class honours degree, having recently been diagnosed with cancer, which must have affected his studies. The Education Department approached me: would I be willing to hold a graduation ceremony for Ron in the prison? In other words, would I celebrate a man who was certainly a murderer?

What would you have done in the case of Gary? Why?
What would you have done with respect to Ron's case? Why?

PART 2

I passed Gary's application on to our Enrolments Section for processing. I am still not sure why. Part of my decision was to do with the comfort of rules: there was no specific reason to reject the application apart from my personal distaste for Gary and potential difficulties with the tutors. I was suspicious, but also not sure of Gary's motive in wanting to study child psychology. I had to consider what my reaction would have been if he had wanted to study, for example, maths or philosophy. Perhaps he was wanting to understand more about himself as a child and what had driven him to behave as he did. In any case, I could not let my personal bias interfere in my decision. The comfort of rules was not a particularly noble reason for a decision, I guess.

Another part of my decision was to support the prison education department. If it makes life easier for them, then that is worth doing. They had been enormously supportive in helping other students in taking our courses. Perhaps there was also a creeping idealism. Maybe – just maybe – Gary could be reclaimed in some way. He was unlikely to ever be released, but perhaps the study might redeem him.

There are limits to what I can manage, though. I would not have him getting any kind of sick charge out of a course that deals with children. He could take introductory, social, cognitive, behavioural – any kind of psychology but child psychology.

So Gary started on his studies, and he turned out to be a reasonably good student. He passed a steady stream of courses and although no tutor warmed to him, no one refused to teach him. Until, that is, Emma. Emma – wouldn't you know it? – was an ex-primary school head teacher. She had worked with young children all her life. She was also a most level headed, down to earth, unflappable woman and experienced tutor. But we all have our break points. 'A man,' said Clint Eastwood, 'has got to know his limitations.' So do women, and Emma knew hers. 'No, I can't do it,' she said. 'I find the man totally repugnant – it's painful to be in the same room with him. I will do it if you really want me to. But I'll hate every moment.'

Gary was one of our students and as such was entitled to tutorial support just like any other. Would I ask Emma to continue to tutor him, trading on her sense of duty and commitment?

I let her off. She agreed to tutor him through extended correspondence but not go into prison any more. I do not feel bad about this decision. She was an excellent tutor and I really had no right to exploit her. But curiously there was a hint of disappointment in her response when I told her she never needed to see Gary again. Perhaps there was almost a sense in which she wanted the challenge, like an adrenaline junky attached to a bungee – wanting to jump yet hating themselves for wanting to. Or perhaps I made that all up – I will never know.

In terms of Ron, it was not much of a conundrum. We held a graduation ceremony in the prison chapel. I dolled up in my impressive but second-rate degree gown and hood and we pinned Ron into a university gown borrowed from one of our tutors.

There was a good turnout – the prison governor and his staff, the chaplain, the whole Education Department, many of the other students, and… the prison Public Relations Office. This threw me. One of my colleagues in another prison had been photographed at a similar ceremony for the most notorious female murderer in the country, a woman whose every doing was salacious feed for the tabloid press. My colleague received more strife for that than anything he had ever done. Our conventional students were the most indignant: they really did not want to be seen to be sharing a qualification with such a person. For a moment I hesitated. But Ron was not notorious, just a run of the mill murderer, and it felt right to go ahead.

I did my little speech as vice-chancellor, university secretary and honorary panjandrum all rolled into one – quite impressively I thought. Then Ron spoke. His parents had been allowed to visit for the day and were guests of honour, sitting in the front row: his dad diminutive in an unaccustomed suit, his mum round, proud and apprehensive. Ron thanked everyone, giving rightful credit to the Education Department, whose commitment to their prisoners is quite humbling. Then he said that this was the first time in his life that he had ever been a credit to his Mum and Dad and burst into tears. He was not the only one – there were tears in the eyes of quite a few of the tough looking audience as we processed out.

There is no moral to this story: Ron was due for release, but it was recently discovered that his cancer had recurred. He was treated in hospital (chained to his bed as is the custom in this civilized country), but his cancer was inoperable. He was finally released on compassionate grounds. But it is not easy to place an ex-murderer: in the end he found a final home in a hospice especially set up for the excluded by a woman who had been imprisoned, raped and tortured by a military regime in South America – the truest Christian I know about.

Ron made the final escape last year. I do not know if he was truly redeemed in any way, but I think he was. Whatever he did to deserve his sentence, I hope it is forgiven him. Who knows what he might have been in a different universe?

CASE REPORTER'S DISCUSSION

As teachers, we are all emotionally involved in our teaching. Indeed we probably would not be very good teachers if we were not. Such involvement means that we are able to develop rapport and trust with our students, that we can, to some extent, understand our students and where they are with their learning. But sometimes those emotions can get in the way of doing an appropriate job. Equally, we all have value systems that underpin our whole approach to life; we need those values to inform our teaching and approach to students. But again, conflict can occur when we meet someone whose values are very different from our own. Some values that we could consider include the value of education, the sanctity of human life, the importance of doing things democratically. On a lower plane, our values may concern punctuality, free expression of emotions and dressing smartly. As teachers, I imagine that we would all have experienced modest conflict from contact with someone whose values in these areas are different from our own.

Gary's case brought issues of values into sharp focus for me. My emotional response to Gary was certainly a factor in considering his application. Indeed, my involvement was the stronger because I had recently become the father of a little girl myself. It was no use taking the old line of 'hating the crime, not the criminal'. Not only was Gary's crime of a peculiarly foul nature, but Gary himself was a sly, manipulative, devious man with no redeeming features at all that I could see. But in the end it seemed to me that my feelings should not be a factor in accepting his application. Ultimately, if we as university teachers cannot be objective, then who can?

In Gary's case, there were fundamental value conflicts as well. Here was someone for whom the sanctity of life seemed to be secondary to his own needs. But I had to contend with the issue of whether this was reason for denying him access to education. His punishment had been decided by the courts – did I have a right to add to that punishment? In facing my situation, I had to consider if there was in fact anyone from history to whom I would deny that chance. Applying it to another situation, I considered the case if Adolf Hitler had been captured alive and imprisoned. Would I have passed his application on? I then asked myself how I would act if the crime had actually been committed against me; would I still allow the application to go through? (As a matter of fact Hitler did try to kill me with a flying bomb on my first birthday in 1945, so it was a good test.) Reflecting on these situations, I came to the realization that yes, I think I would let the applications go forward in all circumstances. My bottom line was that if there was some spark in the person that valued education, then it must be fanned into life. There was always the chance that education might have been the means through which Gary could find a higher purpose in life, to look beyond himself to the sanctity of others. I now believe that it is a very personal issue, and of course others may have different responses.

Having arrived at my stance and accepted the application, I then had to consider if I was entitled to force my values onto someone else by asking them to teach Gary. It is at this point that my resolve runs out. As the supervisor, I have the right to ask them, but if they show any reluctance, then I feel bound not to apply any pressure. But if I take this as a general principle, how far does it extend? If, for instance, I had a student with particular religious beliefs that a tutor found unacceptable and the tutor therefore would not teach the student, what would I do?

Another issue concerns my decision to prevent Gary from studying child psychology. My first response was that his interest was malevolent and sinister. In this light, I certainly responded in an emotional rather than intellectual way. If I had reflected more on his interest from an objective stance, I might have considered that it was based on good intentions. Perhaps he had been brutalized as a child and was seeking ways to come to terms with his experiences and his behaviour, to understand himself. Furthermore, he may not have been interested in cognitive psychology. Perhaps consultation with other professionals with an interest in Gary's case might have assisted me in my decision. As it stands, though, I was not prepared to take the chance and think that, given the circumstances, I made the right decision.

In Ron's case, in deciding that the graduation ceremony should go ahead, I felt I was on more solid ground. I liked Ron. He was friendly and funny and had done a great job supporting other students. But prisoners are notoriously manipulative, and they are well able to hide their feelings and put on a false front to visitors. There was another difference between him and Gary: I did not know what Ron had done to be in prison. If it had been a crime like Gary's, might I have felt differently? I do not know. Neither had I a way of telling whether his values had changed in prison. It was certainly perfectly possible that had Ron been released from prison he would have reverted to type immediately, as so many ex-prisoners do, and assaulted or murdered, or whatever it was he had done.

In the end I made my judgement on what I could see. Here was a man who *as far as I could tell* had acknowledged his offence, had turned his life around and found a peace in using his skills to help others. That was worth celebrating. I am glad we did.

CHAPTER 4

THE PERSONAL IS THE PROFESSIONAL

Case reporter: Sonia Thompson

Issues raised

This case raises the issues of supporting students from groups that have traditionally been discriminated against, and dealing with a subsequent reaction from others in the class.

Background

The events in this case took place approximately nine years ago. The case writer, a lecturer in Community and Youth Studies at a UK college of higher education, was 29 years old and had several years' experience of teaching adults and training. The students had a median age of about 35. The class in focus was studying the subject of social justice.

PART 1

The theoretical part of the unit, sociology, was being taught by Sharon Clarey, a tutor from another department. I was organizing the college-based training and reflective aspects, with contributions from part and full-time teaching staff. We would spend two full days on each of the six following areas: an introduction to understanding social exclusion, class, disability, gender, 'race' and sexuality.

I had already taught this group for two other sessions. Although they had a number of strengths (including a wide range of experiences in the voluntary and statutory sectors, and an ability to engage in work, which they found interesting), they struggled at working consistently and constructively with one another. Moreover, some of them could not work at all with those they did not personally like. This was despite their understanding that such skills are required for effective performance in the field. Small groups often assembled around a shared form of social exclusion. They complained about the attitudes and behaviours of those who they thought were not as 'enlightened' as they were about that particular issue. For example, working class students might speak derogatorily about middle class people. Sometimes the aim of a teaching session would be circumvented by one set of students taking the higher ground over another. Unfortunately, only on rare occasions did a supportive milieu for the sharing of ideas develop.

The crunch came during the two days' input on sexuality. Experienced teachers know only too well that one of the most difficult areas of teaching is to manage learning around the area of sexuality. In general terms, many people rank class, race and gender inequality of greater significance than disability and sexuality. We had tried and tried to persuade groups that we did not believe in a hierarchy of oppressions and that each individual could only speak about and order inequality as a result of their own experiences of social exclusion.

I was very conscious of the complex group dynamics and so I chose to work with a very experienced youth and community worker (Ruth Blake). I knew that her knowledge and background in group work and the profession would be invaluable in shaping the exercises and methods we would use over the two days. We worked over several weeks to sort out how we would best help the students to develop as effective practitioners.

The first day was good. The students considered things like: definitions of sex and sexuality; feminist understandings of sexuality and gender relations; the effects of their personal values around same sex/different sex partners and community and youth work interventions; interactions with young people and community groups; legislation designed to outlaw the 'promotion' of positive images of gay relationships by local authorities. Sally was typical of the students who had earlier expressed concerns about the workshops. She said to me, 'That session went really well. I learnt a lot.' I thought that the group seemed finally to be gelling and they were looking forward to the next day's facilitation.

On the second day, we divided the group along gender lines. We told the women and men students of the exercises they needed to do. Both groups set to work very quickly. It was clear that the learning environment was positive. In fact, it was safe enough for some members of the women's group to disclose their sexuality. Despite this, some of the heterosexual women responded very negatively. So Ruth and I challenged heterosexist and homophobic statements, but it was not long before recriminations started to be exchanged between group members about past statements and behaviours. 'Why should I support your choice of lifestyle when you can't even support me when these things are discussed about class?', Cheryl blurted to Phoebe.

Although Ruth and I initially led the responses to these statements, the usually quiet members soon gained confidence and those who did not agree with the traditionally most vocal group members took command. In this arena we also encouraged participants to relate personal and wider social beliefs on sexuality to the social exclusion that may be experienced by young gay men and young lesbians and community members attempting to use their agency's services. Those with an open mind were willing to reflect upon their own views and practices, while others were too busy expressing disgust to consider the ways in which their values might affect their ability to provide an acceptable level of service to all young people and communities.

Ruth and I found the session extremely difficult and energy-draining. We had to challenge simplistic and offensive answers and to question the assumption that workers can separate personal views from practice, particularly when service development was involved. We had to think carefully about what we would do to improve the situation.

What do you think they should do?
What would you do if you were in this situation?

PART 2

Thankfully, the second workshop seemed to go better. Almost everyone had participated in the two sessions, and we seemed to have made a breakthrough in at least revealing some of the most unpleasant attitudes and beliefs of some group members. This allowed such views to be challenged, rather than remain hidden, only to be perpetuated in the workplace. Several students told us that the session had tackled a number of very difficult issues in a supportive manner.

At the end of each term, unit leaders evaluate the units for which they have responsibility. The information is written up and forms part of a larger report, which is presented and discussed in Course Committee and other Quality Assurance committees. I thought we had done an extremely good job in very difficult circumstances, and looked forward to the evaluation.

We set aside a morning for the evaluation. The students were provided with a copy of unit details, including its aims, objectives, contents and teaching/learning methods. We encouraged them to break into smaller groups to discuss and then evaluate specific aspects of the course. We aimed to write the responses onto flipchart paper, for wider consideration.

When the students had completed their small-group discussions they began to provide feedback. All went well until a spokesperson from one group started. The discussion proceeded as follows.

Sue   Well, the whole thing was a farce. It was rubbish, touchy-feely psychological mumbo-jumbo, especially all that lesbian and homosexuality. I don't see why we were exposed to that kind of nonsense and it's got nothing to do with the real world. Where I work we don't get involved in all that stuff. It's just what I expected from *this* course.

Me   What do you mean? All youth and community workers have to think about their work and how those they work with find them. If you don't reflect on your values and think about the way they influence your work, how will you ever know that your work is effective? How do you expect to work with people and communities if....

Dan   I think Sue's right. The days were just an opportunity for people to get one another back. We never really got anything sorted and...

Me   But its aim wasn't to 'get things sorted'. You just couldn't expect to do that in a few days. It's supposed to introduce you to specific issues, so that you can think about the way that your values have been influenced by wider society, and what sort of impact those values could have on the way you work.

Mary Well, it never worked!

(Sniggers from some of the group)

Me   Well, can you tell me what you have learnt as a result of the workshops? Then we can focus in on the specific areas of the evaluation.

Sue   Yeah. I can honestly say that it was one of the worst experiences of my life. I haven't learnt a thing! All that stuff on sexuality! It was disgusting. That sort of thing has got nothing to do with youth and community work.

Led by a very vocal few, the evaluation quickly descended into a litany of what was wrong with the workshops, the course and the other students.

- The sessions were unnecessary, unpleasant, and made the 'normal' students feel bad about themselves and their attitudes.
- Certain students felt 'oppressed' by having to engage with the material, which they experienced as threatening and distasteful.
- The same students already considered themselves perfectly competent workers and viewed their time in college as merely a hurdle that they were forced to jump in order to get more money for the work which they enjoyed doing.
- Thus they had no intention of changing what they considered to be perfectly acceptable views and working practices.

● If there were any faults, then they clearly lay at the feet of the course, the teaching staff and a few powerful people in the community and youth work field who wanted to force unwholesome ideas on them.

Attempts to involve others in the debate did not prove very successful. Those students who had revealed rising self-confidence in the training sessions remained silent. Few were willing to discuss their positive learning experiences, even though several had already informed me of how constructive the workshops had been for them.

In the past, other teaching staff had informed me of the difficulties they had encountered with the students who agreed to be the spokespeople for their groups, and I had forgotten the extent of the concerns they had expressed. The evaluation left me humiliated and hurt. I had tried and failed to convince the group of the need to be a reflective practitioner. I was caught off-guard and my face must have revealed my defensive feelings. I quickly stopped engaging in discussion with the group and allowed the most vocal within the group to continue with their onslaught and recriminations about the work that had been done. The second stage of the evaluation focused on the theoretical/sociological components of the unit, and by contrast the same students who had just been very vociferous in their criticisms heaped praise on all aspects of the teaching and learning process. Sue's statement as follows was illustrative of the views of this group.

Sue   This is the only part of the course that I've got any time for. It's the only thing I've learnt since I've started this course.

Immediately after the 'evaluation' was completed, several of the quieter students stated that they did not agree with what had been said about the workshops and that they had indeed learnt a great deal from them. They felt unable to say anything supportive within the larger group because they feared an aggressive response from several other group members.

How do you explain the negative reaction?
How would you respond to this situation?

PART 3

I soon realized that I had miscalculated what had been occurring within the workshop sessions. I had assumed that when the traditionally less vocal members of the group had made greater contributions to the workshops, this had been a turning point in group dynamics and personal-professional development. I had failed to understand the extent to which those same individuals would need support and encouragement to continue to make their voices heard in other arenas. Indeed, I had relied on their willingness and ability to contribute in a meaningful way to the unit evaluation. Clearly, I had been overly ambitious and had not taken enough account of group dynamics following the workshops. I had assumed that the less confident students would continue to develop self-esteem outside of the workshop arena; I had not checked out actual group dynamics. My response to the situation was not very constructive. I dwelt on the topic for some time but was soon taken over by the teaching schedule, which provided little opportunity to take the issues further. I did not confront the most critical students or talk with the less confident students, though I did reflect in great detail about my role within the whole process. At the time, I was very demoralized and questioned my ability to teach, especially issues around practice and reflection. However, I did vow to do everything in my power to avoid this type of situation occurring again, either to myself or other students within the group.

CASE REPORTER'S DISCUSSION

In the aftermath of the evaluation I reflected on what had happened, why it happened and how to avoid it ever happening again. Several weeks were committed to being angry with myself, primarily because I had not anticipated the responses that I got. I was infuriated by those within the class who had failed to speak up and let their voices be heard (but were prepared to whisper dissension from the group evaluation in private). The group's past behaviour should have helped me to predict the reaction; I had essentially fallen short and failed to pick up on it.

What had I done to promote or contribute to such a destructive evaluation? Was there any merit in some of what the students had identified? Should the sessions merely focus on behaviour and not values? There is a school of thought which suggests that values are personal matters and that employers/trainers and so on should focus in on what people do, rather than what they think. Organizations can therefore demand that particular behaviours are undertaken and others not followed. No attempt is made to identify what employees believe, or to affect the way they think. On the other hand they would experience difficulty dealing with attitudes, which were often 'invisible' and difficult to measure. Is it better therefore to invest in behaviour rather than attitude change?

If I as a tutor felt so unhappy and despondent in this situation, how might students within the group have felt? Do they have to go through this sort of negative response on a regular basis? Aware of students' need for personal assistance, student-led support groups had been timetabled to occur on a weekly basis. Why were the groups not working? What could be done to stop this very negative and destructive behaviour within the group? Did any systems or structures exist which could deal with the very destructive behaviour displayed by some group members?

Reflecting on the episode confirmed rather than weakened my belief that community and youth work students must contemplate all aspects of their practice, and this includes being clear about how personal values can affect professional practice. I still think that it is essential to explore and identify the boundaries of beliefs and professional practice. To what extent can a racist offer meaningful support to a black young person? What sort of advice and information can a misogynist give a community-based women's group? Would a eugenicist be able to assist a coalition of disabled people to lobby for their needs within the community? Religion, strangely enough, has never been a barrier to effective and supportive youth and community work practice. For example, several practising Christians have found a way to marry their religious and personal value system with support for the needs of gay and lesbian communities.

The debate reminds us that all of our views (and those of any professional body) are, and should be, subjected to examination and challenge. However, in the long run, when personal beliefs are in conflict with professional values, a choice between the personal philosophy and career might have to be made. I guess that is the crunch. It was obviously good for those students for whom there was a personal experience, but for others, they did not make the connection between their professional practice and beliefs. Surely that would provide very rich ground for discussion. Can you be a good practitioner and bigot at the same time? It is a very interesting question, as one person's bigotry is another's religion. So 'being clear' may in fact be a legitimately contested area – or at least some students thought this, and were not convinced otherwise.

I believe that the group work that Ruth and I engaged in had many positive effects, allowing the less confident group members to participate and get their views heard. This, alongside the gender split, did however provide many with 'too safe a space' within which to consider whether or not to share aspects of their sexuality. I say this because the responses to their statements were overtly heterosexist and homophobic. Although the women who disclosed aspects of their lives have all said that that they felt that they had made the right decision, I still struggle with balancing group work (which increases safety within a group) alongside the capacity of group members to use sensitive material in a negative manner.

My evaluations are now more methodical and students are given greater guidelines within which to operate. There is clarity about what counts as valid and invalid feedback, and minority views must be allowed to be heard. The student-led support groups were evaluated and dropped from the new course. Individuals were finding their own support, often from outside their own cohort. When the course came up for revalidation, the decision was taken to build in a personal skills audit and action plan. Students had to assess their levels of self-confidence and speaking in groups, and develop appropriate action plans. The new course also builds in opportunities for the less confident students to practise speaking in the larger group. All students are required to chair a student meeting, to develop and deliver a presentation and to participate in general classroom activities.

I am also much clearer now that it is not possible to control all elements of the teaching–learning context, nor is it desirable to do so. A certain degree of uncertainty is a necessary part of the developmental process, not just for students, but also for teaching staff!

CHAPTER 5

INTERCULTURAL INEXPERIENCE

Case reporters: Zhu Yunxia and Jacqueline Harrison

Issues raised

This case study raises the issue of intercultural miscommunication, exacerbated by body language. It focuses on appropriate use of gestures when communicating with students from a different culture, and investigates specific strategies for conflict resolution in academic teaching and learning.

Background

The incident in this case study took place in the mid-1990s in a communication course for office administration students in a large polytechnic in New Zealand. The class comprised 25 students, of whom 12 were Chinese from mainland China. Most of the Chinese students were new immigrants and had been in New Zealand for less than a year. The teacher, Rita, had more than 20 years' teaching experience and had taught English in several countries. However, this was the first time that she had taught Chinese students. The teacher was in her forties and the students were in their twenties.

PART 1

'Oh no, not that phone again!' I silently fumed as I struggled to complete the paper due for presentation at a conference the day after next. Calming myself, I picked up the receiver. Answering professionally, I was surprised to hear Margaret, the head of department, on the other end. She sounded concerned.

A group of Chinese students in my subject had recently complained about my teaching, and she wanted to know from me directly what had led to the complaint. I was amazed! How could this be, when I thought everything was going fine? I was enjoying teaching the subject and nothing important had ever gone wrong before. The students appeared to be responding to the major issues covered in class. In particular I liked the international nature of the class, with students from Korea, Japan, China and Russia. Although some students' language skills were not very good, they seemed to be trying their best to meet the requirements of the assessments. What was more, they brought their own cultural flavours into my class. One student, for example, showed Chinese artefacts used to celebrate the Lunar New Year.

So I assumed that the 'complaint' must be the result of some form of misunderstanding and thought, 'I must get to the bottom of this.' It was then that I started to recall what had happened between me and the group of Chinese students lately.

As recent immigrants, this group had some difficulty with their English. However, they were very keen to learn and they were always polite and respectful. But when I thought about it more carefully, I realized that there was something odd going on. Sometimes they spoke Chinese among themselves during class. I did not have a clue what they were talking about and nor did the other students.

For example, in a recent tutorial I had been going over some of the details regarding the report, which was the major written assessment for this semester. I had started by looking at and explaining the objective for this piece of assessment and the marking criteria. The students suddenly started talking in Chinese! As I had done when this had occurred previously, I asked the students to speak in English if they wanted to discuss any point. Although they nodded, they stopped talking immediately. Trying to come to terms with this event, I thought that they might not have understood my explanation and so I went over some of the important points again.

As soon as we finished the class, Lan, the most capable speaker of English within the group, who seemed to have assumed the role of the representative for the Chinese students, approached me. She asked for further details about this particular piece of assessment, the report. At this point, the rest of the group began to gather around me and appeared to be listening intently to the discussion. I was perplexed. Why had they asked me again about the information on the report assignment that I had just given them twice in class? In fact, I felt a little impatient with having to repeat the information again, but was sure that I had not conveyed this to Lan.

Hiding my perplexity, I asked Lan in the normal tone I had used in class, 'Lan, can you please be more specific about what you want to know regarding the assessment?'

'We are not very clear about the marking criteria,' she replied. 'For example, what are we supposed to include in the introduction? There are so much things we may want to look at.' Clearly, her question was not very specific. For general questions like this one, the answers could be found in the course guide. There was no need for me to repeat what was detailed there.

Tossing the course guide to Lan, I replied, 'I gave a very detailed explanation of what I required for this assessment, and all the information in relation to marking criteria can be found on page 12 of the course guide.' However, I added, 'Please come back to me again if you still have questions after reading the course guide.'

Flushing slightly, Lan responded in a much lower voice, but clear enough for everyone to hear, 'Yes. I know. But it would be good if you can explain this once again to us. You know that our English is not very good.'

With an even greater effort to control my impatience, I said, 'I would really appreciate it a lot if all of you can read carefully once again the marking criteria for this task in the course guide.'

Once again, the Chinese students nodded, their faces expressionless. I could not tell whether they had understood my explanation. Without another word, they filed out of the classroom.

I do not know why, but the phone call from my head of department seemed to reactivate this event in my mind. I began to reflect on what I had said and done on that day, and why the students had reacted the way they did. I really was perplexed.

What do you think is going on here?
Why do you think the Chinese students were speaking Chinese to each other in class?
What do you think the teacher should do next?
What do you think actually happened?

PART 2

After hearing my side of the story, Margaret suggested that we meet with the students to hear their concerns directly. Since there were 12 students involved, we met in a classroom, with the chairs arranged in a circle. The students seemed reluctant to attend a meeting with me present. They stood around awkwardly, and when Margaret invited them to sit down, they chose the chairs farthest away from me, and avoided eye contact.

Margaret began the meeting by asking the students to outline their concerns. The students looked uncomfortable. Thinking that they might feel more at ease without me in the room, I offered to step outside. Margaret, however, wanted me to stay. 'In New Zealand,' she said, 'we like to address difficulties in an open way. It is important for us all to know exactly and directly what the problem is, so that we can all work on finding some common ground.' The students looked disappointed, perhaps because they did not have the opportunity to speak with Margaret alone.

After a pause, Lan spoke up. 'I am the speaker for the group,' she declared.

'Are you all happy to have Lan speak for you?' asked Margaret. The students turned towards Lan and there was a brief exchange in Chinese. They then turned back to Margaret and nodded. I was feeling extremely embarrassed and wished that Margaret had agreed to let me leave before.

In halting English, Lan summarized the student perspective. I was horrified! Apparently I had not only offended the students deeply by my gesture in tossing the course guide, but my remarks had been interpreted as insulting. The students wanted me removed as their teacher. 'We think you should fire her, because we cannot learn from her.'

'No!' said Margaret. 'This is not how we resolve issues in New Zealand.' She then attempted to explain the need for natural justice, and for all parties to a dispute to be heard. However, I could see that the students were having trouble understanding both the concept and Margaret's words. They grew increasingly restive. 'I am certain that Rita did not intend to offend or insult you. Rita…'

Taking this as my cue, I attempted to apologize for my clumsy actions.

However, the students were adamant. 'We do not attend any more classes while she is the teacher,' said Lan.

The meeting reached an impasse. The students refused to consider that there was any other option besides removing me from their class. Margaret was equally firm that this was not an option. Eventually, she was forced to end the meeting, and the students left, looking just as unhappy as they had when the meeting started.

Margaret and I then went to her office to discuss the situation. I could not think of a way out, other than to have someone else take over my class. Although I was grateful for Margaret's support in keeping me on, I felt both depressed and inadequate.

What would you do now if you were the head of department?
What would you do now if you were the teacher?
What do you think actually happened next?

PART 3

The first meeting did not get us anywhere. Clearly we had to change our communication style. It was Margaret who suggested that we might bring in a mediator and then organize a further meeting with the Chinese students. We decided that the best person to play this role was Jin Ling, who was also a teacher in our department. Jin Ling was Chinese, and had been in Australia for five years before coming to New Zealand two years previously. She also had taught in Chinese and Australian institutions. Although neither Margaret nor I attended the meeting, we learnt from Jin Ling later on that her meeting with the students had been very successful. Here is what Jin Ling told us.

It was a pleasant meeting. Most of the 12 Chinese students arrived punctually at 8.30 am. They greeted me politely, and Lan asked me a few questions about myself, such as when I arrived in this country. I answered each question politely. The meeting was conducted in English because the programme leader was also present.

I started the meeting by introducing our major objective, which was to seek common ground between the teacher and the Chinese students. On hearing this, the students' smiles immediately disappeared. Lan once again was the first one to speak. She said it was impossible to work out common ground because the conflict between them and Rita was too great and had gone on too long. Then she illustrated in detail how Rita 'threw' the course guide at her.

All this confirmed my suspicion. I began to realize how true it was that the conflict was triggered by that non-verbal gesture. They told me that Rita had been disrespectful to them because she thought that they were stupid. Then they listed a few other incidents such as being reluctant to answer their questions, as associated with the 'disrespectful' attitude.

I asked, 'Do you think there may be some kind of misunderstanding between you and your teacher? I know it is hard for you,' I continued, 'but perhaps we should ponder over this issue again and explore a possible common ground?'

They agreed that there was no common ground because they were not treated with appropriate respect. I was really surprised to hear them say this so assuredly. However, I suggested, 'Maybe we can think about alternative ways of solving the problem. Perhaps the best option is to think from a different perspective.'

'A different perspective? What do you mean by this?' Lan's eyes lit up.

I explained, 'The new perspective is an intercultural perspective. Let's think about the differences we may encounter when we communicate with people across cultures. Everyone tends to view the world from his/her own perspective which is very much culturally defined. Your teacher perhaps didn't mean to insult anyone when she tossed the course guide, and this gesture can be accepted as relaxed and informal in New Zealand. However, it may cause misunderstanding and can be interpreted as an insult by people from another culture which stresses formality.'

There was silence and hesitation among the group. They looked at each other, not knowing what to say.

I grasped the opportunity and asked whether it was possible to consider reconciling and going back to class since there had been a misunderstanding. However, I explained to them that I wouldn't try to press them for a response, and they could decide whenever they were ready.

To my great surprise, after a few minutes' discussion among the group, they came up with this decision: 'Yes'. They were prepared to reconcile and go back to class if I would agree to sit in on classes too.

Do you think it is appropriate to invite a mediator to help solve the problem? What would you do if you were in this position? What do you think happened next?

PART 4

In the following week after the meeting, Jin Ling was with us in class. Her original role as a mediator diminished. Instead, she became a kind of additional teacher and a friend to the students. I was very happy to see the improvement that the group of Chinese students were making every day. Generally speaking, they were more responsive in class and their discussion was carried out in English most of the time. By the end of the semester, they also improved their scores, and in particular, the scores of the reporting writing assessment.

One month after the end of the semester, I received a phone call from Lan, who surprised me with this news: she had found a job and now was working as an administrator in Auckland. She concluded her call by asking me whether it was possible to discuss further differences between New Zealand and Chinese cultures. I was thrilled to hear from her. Of course I would be more than happy to help. What had happened was a learning curve in developing intercultural competency. However, we still have a lot to learn in our new intercultural experience.

How satisfactory do you think the outcome was for the students, for the teacher and for the department?
How important was it that the mediator had such a good understanding of the different cultures involved?
Do you think there is anything that should have been done differently?

CASE REPORTERS' DISCUSSION

The predominant issues in this case study concern appropriate use of non-verbal messages and the employment of effective strategies for conflict resolution in a multicultural environment.

Why and how did Rita get herself into the conflict she describes? It appears that the gesture of tossing the course guide, which was intended to convey a relaxed informality, instead was interpreted by the students as a serious insult. The tension between Rita and the students then clearly built up from this incident until it evolved into open conflict. So although many of us might pay some attention to verbal communication across cultures when we teach, non-verbal communication is an area in which we may not be so well prepared.

Communicating with students from different cultural backgrounds helps us understand not only other cultures but our own as well. Rita began to reflect on her use of gestures only when the conflict between her and the group emerged. She could have avoided the conflict if she had identified the misunderstanding earlier. However, we tend to accept our ways as normal and right. Only when our behaviour is challenged in an intercultural encounter do we begin to see more clearly the differences among cultures. This is also the process of increasing cultural awareness. Many academics working in a multicultural environment may face similar issues.

Rita was also compelled to seek strategies for resolving conflicts. As the situation unfolded, the first resolution strategy failed, perhaps because the style and power relationships all supported the position of the head of department and teacher. The students still felt aggrieved that their voice was not being heard. The second attempt with the mediator was more successful, presumably because the style of this solution (and the person of the mediator herself) had the trust of both sides.

From the case, Rita and Margaret agreed that the need for a mediator became imperative since the first meeting with the students failed. This move was not recommended in the case as a first priority. The first choice was for the teacher and the students to solve the problem themselves. Not all teachers may have the opportunity of hiring or assuming such a role. However, we may consider when it is the appropriate time to involve a mediator. We may weigh up a series of factors, such as who we are communicating with. The Chinese students in the case did not seem to welcome the confrontational style as employed in the first meeting. This may be the reason why the students changed and improved their attitudes towards the conflict during the second meeting organized by Jin Ling. But we may think about varying our strategies when we communicate with students from other cultures such as German or American.

Margaret seemed to have made a good choice for a mediator. Jin Ling was equipped with an adequate knowledge of both cultures and 'spoke' the cultural language at the meeting, which made it possible for the students to think from a different perspective.

However, enhancing intercultural competency is a continous learning experience for both Rita and the students, as well as for other colleagues, as indicated in the telephone conversation between Rita and Lan. With good intention and relevant cultural awareness from both sides, our competence can be enhanced to a new level in our further intercultural encounters.

Have you or your department organized any basic training to increase cultural awareness and enhance intercultural competence?

Do you know what conciliation service is available on campus if there is such a need?

Does this study have any other implications for teaching international or overseas students?

CHAPTER 6

FREEDOM TO FAIL

Case reporter: Tanya Kantanis

Issues raised

This case raises the issue of bridging the gap between adolescence and adulthood in accepting responsibly for self-directed learning.

Background

This case takes place at a large, multi-campus Australian university. 'Adam', the student, and I, the teacher, had known each other since enrolment at the beginning of the year when I had provided course advice to Adam. Adam was a school leaver, first-year student undertaking an arts/education double degree. As a teacher of 20 years' experience in secondary and tertiary education, I was interested in issues of transition to university, and committed to assisting students in adjusting to the different teaching and learning styles they experience at university.

PART 1

Adam had attended tutorials on a regular basis and had more than met the 80 per cent attendance requirement. Throughout the semester, he had been a regular contributor to this highly diverse and interactive class where students freely expressed their ideas and produced opinions covering a very broad spectrum. On a number of occasions I had been surprised and disturbed by the immaturity (both verbal and non-verbal) that Adam demonstrated.

Essentially, he was highly intolerant of views other than his own. Although I noted this, I chose not to say anything directly to Adam. Instead, when the context permitted, I indicated to the class as a whole that, at university, students were often challenged by peers who came from different backgrounds, had different values and espoused views different from their own. I elaborated further by linking these comments to their future professional lives, in that as teachers they would be likely to face similar challenges in interacting with their own students and students' families. Adam remained unmoved and continued to display the same behaviour.

As the semester progressed, a clear discrepancy became evident. Although Adam had attended and participated on a regular basis, written assessment tasks had not been forthcoming with the same consistency. However, he was not alone in having work that was still outstanding as the semester drew to a close, and I reminded all students of the need to attend to any assessment tasks that had not yet been completed and submitted.

The due dates passed and still Adam did not submit two assessment tasks. I could have easily accepted this situation and failed him for non-submission of work, but this was not my preferred option. Not wishing an otherwise competent student to be denied the opportunity to pass the subject, I tried to contact Adam by phone. Despite several attempts to ring him, I was unsuccessful; no one was at home when I called and there was no answering machine to leave a message. As the time for result submission was drawing nearer, I became increasingly anxious. Given that I regularly communicated with students via e-mail I decided to send a message to Adam in one, final, desperate attempt to get in touch with him. Days passed without any response. What had happened to him? Why was he not responding? I became resigned to the fact that there was nothing further to be done and that I would indeed have to record a 'fail' for Adam due to his lack of completion of two substantial assessment tasks for this subject.

Working late in my office one night, I noticed the mail notification flag pop up on my computer. Adam had finally responded – a wave of relief swept over me. As the e-mail had only just arrived, I called his home immediately, hoping to speak directly to him to explain the urgency of the situation, including the dire consequences that would follow if he chose not to submit the outstanding assessment tasks. This time, to my relief, after a few short rings the phone was picked up. A male voice, not Adam's, answered. I asked to speak to Adam, only to be told that he was not at home. I enquired whether the person at the other end of the line could please pass on a message for Adam to contact me. This seemingly innocent request had the effect of making the other party (Adam's father) an interrogator worthy of the Spanish Inquisition! Who was this woman who wanted his son to contact her? Why was the matter so urgent that she would call after 'business hours'? I thought that I would allay the father's concerns by telling him I was his son's tutor in subject X, but this only resulted in another barrage of questions. Finally,

I relented and indicated that the matter was indeed 'work related', reiterating that I needed to speak to Adam as soon as possible. On this note the conversation ended. Confident that I had been able to communicate the urgency of the matter, I expected Adam to contact me the following day.

Was the phone call to Adam appropriate?
Why do you think Adam's father reacted so strongly to the phone call?
What do you think happened next?

PART 2

Sure enough, Adam did send me an e-mail the following day. An exchange of e-mails ensued, the relevant sections of which I have included here. The first e-mail from Adam read:

Dear Tanya,
I apologize for the lateness of this work and any inconvenience that it may have caused. As you can obviously understand, with exams present this work did not take a priority.

Thank you for your understanding, and hopefully if all goes to plan, I will be able to either drop off in your pigeon hole or e-mail the reading exercise today.

Again thanks, for the time and understanding.

However, let me just say one more thing. I appreciate the fact that you went out of your way to attempt to make contact with me on a number of occasions. However, talking to my parents about the outstanding work seems to me inappropriate. I would have liked to think that you could have, in some way, talked to me first, yes it was incredibly late but I have intended to do it all along. Yes, obviously talking to my parents has had the desired effect, but it has discredited the system which has worked so well at uni, in particular, in Education, of treating students as adults and not like children in school still. I understand that this work needed to be completed, yet I still think that in approaching and discussing the problem with my parents you have not given me the credit which you have throughout the semester, along with each and every other student. I understand that I am in the wrong here and in no way am I trying to deny or displace this fact yet I still believe that what I have said is fair and worthy of comment so in future this can be avoided.

I hope that in no way am I out of line in saying this, and I would also like to say that I would not even consider expressing this to any other tutor. It is only that I understand that you will see it the way that it is meant, and that it is not me trying to be a smart-ass or showing you disrespect.

Again, I would like to say that I appreciate your understanding, and appreciate your effort throughout the year, especially with my subject selection.

You may choose to respond to this e-mail if you wish, but in no way am I looking to cause any trouble therefore I would not be offended if you were not to respond.

Thank you,

Adam

I was aghast that my intentions had been so misconstrued. In endeavouring to assist this student, I had inadvertently set in motion a chain of events that I could never have predicted. My innocent call to Adam's home had resulted in the father inferring that my motive in attempting to contact his son was less than honourable, and while my explanation of who I was appeased the father, it infuriated the son. Despite the fact that Adam and I shared a good rapport, and he acknowledged I treated my students as adults at all times, he did not pause to consider any scenario other than the one he presumed was the case: that I had called his home with the express purpose of speaking to his parents. Not only did I feel humiliated by the father, now I was being judged unfairly by Adam. I felt hurt and angry. I had, after all, tried to help this student and this was his thanks. Of course I had to reply.

Dear Adam,

Thank you for sending the teaching procedures…

As to the other matter, I think you have misinterpreted the situation. The reason I called immediately upon receiving your e-mail was to speak to YOU to find out if there was something untoward that had occurred which prevented you from completing the set work. It most certainly was NOT my intention to speak to your parents. I assumed that as I'd just received the e-mail, that you would be home and (given that I hadn't been able to speak to you earlier and it was late Thursday that you were responding to the e-mail I had sent early Monday morning) this would be the ideal time to catch up with you.

After being told that you were not at home, I attempted to leave my name and number but your father was very firm in finding out who I was and what business I had calling you.

I am sorry if this has caused tension for you at home. With hindsight, perhaps I should not have attempted to make contact with you regarding the work but simply allowed you, as a truly independent learner, the 'freedom to fail' due to non-submission, as this would appear to be your more preferred option. I can see that even with the best of intentions I have received your wrath.

Regards,
Tanya

Immediately upon receipt of this e-mail, Adam responded:

Dear Tanya,
I apologize that I have created a situation where it seems that you feel that I am ungrateful for the effort and care that you have shown to ensure that I will not fail. I, in no circumstances, ever intended to give that impression. However, my thought was to tell you that I would have preferred for you to deal with me in the situation. Yet hearing what you have said, I am happy to admit that I may have jumped the gun a little, automatically presuming that you rang with the intention of talking to my parents. However, as this was not the case I cannot be unimpressed with the course of action that you took. Therefore, I shall endeavour to finish this work and e-mail it to you as soon as possible. I am sorry if I gave the impression of harsh feeling or resentment, but take what I have said in the following way in which it was meant. I came to expect of you a level of respect, (ie you treating your students as adults) therefore, I was, as it turns out, a little too quick to respond.

Therefore I am sorry that I have questioned your good intentions, and was a little too quick to blame others, when really I have brought this upon myself.

I will no doubt talk to you later in the day.
Thank you again,
Adam

Adam did complete and submit the outstanding work in time for it to be assessed. He passed the subject and proceeded to second year. This incident did not adversely affect our relationship; in subsequent years when we encountered one another, greetings were always pleasantly exchanged and there was no sign of animosity.

CASE REPORTER'S DISCUSSION

I believe that both Adam and I learnt valuable lessons from this experience. Adam was an immature young man when he commenced university. The outcome of his prior schooling was to confirm the view that he was competent and confident: this is clearly demonstrated by his cavalier attitude and presumptuous response to the situation. What he was not prepared for when he came to university was to be a self-directed learner responsible for his own actions (and inactions). It could be argued that I did not foster this through my intervention, but I do not believe that the first-year university experience should be a matter of throwing students in at the deep end to see who survives and who does not. Adam was a competent student who was more than capable of completing the subject successfully. The question for me was, should he be penalized for poor time management and a lack of organizational skills?

My actions, which I do not regret, plainly indicate my view on this matter. Adam deserved the opportunity to progress through his course without the encumbrance of 'overloading' in the following year or extending the completion time of his course. His response was entirely in keeping with the immaturity that I had already observed to be a part of his character. I should have remembered and accepted that, and maintained my own objectivity. Instead, I too reacted emotionally rather than rationally when I stated, 'perhaps I should... have... simply allowed you, as a truly independent learner, the freedom to fail due to non-submission, as this would appear to be your more preferred option'. This reflects my frustration and anger, which I regret as it makes me no better than Adam in being quick to judge simply because the response was not what I anticipated. This experience has made me more conscious of giving matters careful consideration rather than hurtling headlong into a response which could easily escalate matters to a crisis.

Adam, too, learnt this salient lesson from the experience: he is now less likely to judge too hastily without being in full possession of the facts. This has profoundly affected his level of maturity. He has made significant progress from late adolescence to early adulthood. He also learnt that respect is earned and not simply a consequence of age, status, power relation and so on. Although I do not doubt that he respected me, this view was challenged temporarily when he thought I had 'betrayed' him, and later reinforced when he understood the reason for my actions.

Adam has matured through this process because I chose not to take the easy option by allowing him the 'freedom to fail', instead recognizing that he was not yet in a position to take on the responsibilities of an adult and as such required some guidance. This has been a valuable lesson for Adam from another perspective. In his chosen profession as a secondary teacher there will often be instances where his own actions and/or words may be misconstrued by the students he teaches – just as mine were by him. Although the issue of confusion between the teacher's message and students' interpretation is a consistent theme in the teaching of Education students, few have the opportunity to learn this lesson through such direct means.

Since this incident occurred, I have continued to contact students at risk of failure due to non-submission of work. I do this irrespective of their competence in the subject. The main means of communication I use these days is e-mail. Aside from obviating the possibility that I will strike, once again, an obstreperous parent, I like the permanency that written communication provides. As electronic submission, correction and return of work is the norm for my students, they do not see an e-mail reminder as anything other than the ongoing dialogue we share about their work.

Over the course of the academic year, I get to know my students well. (First-year Education subjects are sequential: each class is taught by the same staff member, students remaining in the same class unless a transfer is requested.) Awareness of class dynamics and individual students' personalities creates a positive learning and teaching environment. My experience has been that when students know staff to be receptive and responsive to their needs, they are more collaborative and cohesive as a class, and this generates a culture of mutual respect that is also mutually rewarding. This is significant in a course such as Education, where role-modelling is crucial in demonstrating that being a 'teacher' brings with it serious responsibilities. Being in a position to affect (sometimes irrevocably) the lives of others is an important duty with which 'teachers' have been charged. This needs to be communicated in both overt and covert ways to students. This perception of the learning and teaching nexus, complemented by familiarity with issues of adjustment faced by first-year students, reinforces my belief that it is imperative to assist students at this time of great upheaval in their lives. I do not believe in creating additional obstacles that will make first-year students casualties in their transition to university. I give students much of the freedom they expect to find at university. However, as the majority of students at my institution are school leavers, often not in a position to accept all of the responsibilities that accompany such freedom, I see it as my responsibly to withhold from them the 'freedom to fail'.

CHAPTER 7

LOVELY SHIRLEY

Case reporter: Anonymous

Issues raised

This case raises the issue of miscommunication that can occur in a culturally-diverse setting when the medium for communication is e-mail.

Background

The following incident occurred in a large culturally-diverse university in Australia. The language and academic skills lecturer had been working in the field for 10 years and was in her mid-forties. The student was in his mid-to-late twenties.

PART 1

Although I had been working in the language and learning field for 10 years, I had no experience of Nick's culture. Nick, a student in his mid-to-late twenties, had immigrated recently to Australia from a troubled past life, largely arising from the politics of his country: a South-east Asian nation, subject to internal strife. Nick was also one of the first students I had worked with who had an e-mail account.

It was completely accidental that we met on that day. Although the semester had well and truly started, I had finally found a moment to finish getting materials ready for the year's teaching activities. This mainly involved revising class notes and sorting out the files of those students I had seen for one to one consultations the previous year. I thumbed through the files, working out pretty quickly who was likely to return, and those who had developed enough to have their files safely stashed in the top cupboard. I moved from the filing cabinet to the student resource room, lingering there while I thumbed through the new resources, picking out some materials for the new class I had been asked to run for a third-year computing subject. In the past, the class typically comprised approximately 90 per cent non-English speaking background students, and the lecturer often had problems trying to get the students to understand – and create their own – data commentaries. I was leaning over the books, enjoying the customary challenge of figuring out which ideas to pick up and marry with the subject content.

Suddenly Nick was standing before me. It was late in the day and I was the only one in the centre. He had been told about the special computing class and wanted to get extra help. He was lucky to find me there.

Nick spoke to me generally about his learning needs. He had not been in Australia long and had, in fact, completed a professional degree overseas. To be qualified in Australia, he had to join the course at third-year level. He said he would have no trouble understanding the content of the course, but he was worried about his English. Could I help?

I thought. If I suggested one to one consultations, this would counteract the efficiencies of being able to deal with all the students in a group. He had e-mail, he said, so I could send him information. As he appeared to be a keen and conscientious student, I said that I would e-mail him some references as soon as I could.

He then started asking me what I was doing over the Easter holidays and we chatted for a few minutes more.

When I sent the references the next day, I accompanied it with the cheerful message:

> Thought about your situation for a while, and feel that these references would be the most suitable for you. I'm sure you'll enjoy reading through them and you'll learn a bit about Australian culture. If you buy the grammar book with the exercises I suggested and use it regularly, you'll notice how some of those things you're puzzling over will gradually become a bit clearer. Enjoy your holiday.

For four days, I thought of other things. On the Tuesday, I sat down at my computer and opened my mailbox. Nothing had prepared me for the e-mail I received. The Subject line was 'Lovely ShirLey':

> Hello ShirLey!
> Thanks for your kindness and your response, very very cool when I read your letter. I have to tell you it was very nice when you were wearing a very beautiful necklace. I like it very much. I would like to tell you

about my past life and what I would like to be in the coming future. I am glad to read your letter and I am very proud I meet you in Australia. Although we get a big wall between us which is respect teacher and student as specially you and me. But I wish you understand what I would like to be between us. I was born on 14th December 1961, my parents died in 1993 while I was studying outside my country. I fight for freedom and human rights that's why I left my country. I lost my past life. I am being honest with you. I don't have any relationship here and I have no one to discuss about my future life. I am very lucky because I survive here but unfortunately some of my friends were killed by typhoid or at the battles. I need you who will be my friend but I see the wall which is the lecturer and students to keep. Anyway I would like to talk to you if you wish to listen to my past life and I would like to get some advice. I wish to settle down in Australia so can you advise me about that. My life's very lonely and I really hate what is happening in my life. I didn't feel anything about the Easter holidays because no one had relationship in here so that's why I asked about your holidays. If you will give me a chance I can explain in more detail. I hope I will finish my degree next year when I have the job I would like to see you again.

I am so glad about who's take caring and helping me for my future. I will never forget your sympathy and your kindness.

With Love,

Nick

PS As soon as possible I wish to read your letters.

I sat and stared at the machine. After a while I got up, paced around the room, sat down and stared again. It was really the first non-business e-mail I had received. I had an eerie sense of being inside this student's head. Except, no matter how many times I read and re-read the message, I could not understand what it was saying. It was not the English, though I could not help feeling that, had a preposition been more apt here, a sentence not run together there, I might have gotten closer to the meaning.

Questions were reeling around in my brain, all knocking into each other and falling in a heap, still making no sense. Was it a letter built on some undertaking Nick thought I had given him? If so, was this an offer of friendship? In fact, I had not made mention of any individual tuition, so it could not be about teaching, surely. Or could it – maybe that was what he was asking for? If it was not – in some sense – a romantic letter, why the necklace, the talk of love and of his future plans? What was 'the wall' preventing and how solid did he perceive the wall to be?

Feeling unable to read the situation adequately myself, I sought advice from both my line manager and the counselling service.

What do you think is going on here?
What would be your advice to Shirley?
What do you think happened next?

PART 2

I rang the boss. I did not show him the letter, but extrapolated from it to indicate that I felt uneasy about it and was not sure how to respond. The classes were starting the next day: what was I to do? Phillip, the line manager, had recent experience of 'troublesome' students hassling female staff and felt a hard line needed to be taken. A little concerned for my safety, he asked if I felt I needed any particular support or help. We agreed it would be useful to talk to one of the head counsellors. Phillip suggested one whom I knew already and who had at times been involved in mediating cases where there was a problem between a student and a staff member.

I rang Belinda, the counsellor, explaining that I was in a dilemma about how to respond to the student. I was starting to worry that all this asking was starting to give the case a life of its own. While I might occasionally have compared notes with a colleague, I had never needed to ask for anyone's help with a student. Belinda asked me to send the e-mail so she could evaluate the situation more accurately. I sent it. Belinda rang back in an hour.

> Shirley, people like this develop a fantasy that you have given them indi-
> cations that they are special to you. If you try to talk to this student face
> to face, no matter what you are saying, he will find evidence in a look or
> a word that you feel differently. This is what you need to do: reply by e-
> mail, and state that the relationship for you is exactly the same as for all
> your other students. Make it very clear. Leave no room for doubt.
> Believe me: I've seen this before.

Should I take their advice? Were they right? Were they right that my response should be via e-mail? How come I had spent more than 20 years of a professional life engaging with language and was unable to come to grips with a student e-mail? I felt that it just might be a mixture of cultural and linguistic miscommunication, compounded by the odd tone of familiarity that the e-mail system obviously in some way licensed. But what if I was wrong and they were right? Maybe I should ask Nick to come and see me and explain very gently that I believed he had got the wrong end of the stick. Aside from the embarrassment of this for both of us, what if he started insisting that I had given him encouragement? When my line manager and an experienced student counsellor both thought this was possible, how could I go my own way with any confidence? How could I go back to them and confess I had thought I knew better, but had only succeeded in making the situation worse?

I sent the message:

> Nick
>
> I aim to be empathetic and kind to all the students I teach, and it is important for you to understand that there is nothing more to it than that.
>
> If you need to talk further to anyone, you can contact the Student Counsellor at the following address…

In at my desk the next day, I found two e-mails, the first sent at 6.32 the previous evening:

> Hello!
>
> Thank you very much for your response. I think something is missing in my poor English. I wish to you who seem to be like my sister or my teacher or my mother. You have a lot more experience than me and I accept your advice. I was telling you my past life, that's all. If you are not happy about my words, please understand and forgive me. I always respect your aims and your kindness. I expect this letter would be clear what I wish to be. However I never forget how you offer support for my studying.
>
> Yours sincerely,
> Nick

This surely seemed to point towards misunderstanding. Had he realized that he had unwittingly sent the wrong signal in his first e-mail? Or was it just rewriting history? 'If you are not happy about my words…': had he realized only now perhaps that he had misunderstood my demeanour towards him? Surely he could not have thought that he was talking to me in that e-mail like a sister or a mother, *or* a teacher, for that matter.

The second e-mail had been sent at 10.07 pm:

> Hello!!
> Good day!
> Please try to read this letter, Mrs I. I can't concentrate on my study because I feel so bad until I explain. You are a very nice person and a good teacher who I meet in university.
>
> I am being honest with you.
>
> I am the only son in my family. I always say that my mom and my sisters what they are wearing which is beautiful or not. When I was in high school I told my classmate when she laughed showing her all teeth and came into the classroom, so I said you look like an advertisement

for make-up. When our teacher heard what I said he asked us who said that. When I stood up and told him I did, he asked me again 'Have you ever spoken to your sister like that?' I said that yes I did. After that he expelled me from the classroom. I didn't lie to him. I have a very weak point which is saying true words most of the time. Sometimes it is very bad for me.

Then followed 20 lines touching on his army experiences and outlining the very painful memories he had of war, death and disregard for human rights.

I usually discuss my life with my sisters and my mother when I am there. No one's here with me at the moment. I need to discuss and wish to take advice from the one whose experience is more than mine here and who has a good heart. That's why I wish you look like my mum or sister or teacher. However, you can't accept it. I am very sad for that. Because you don't know me very well and you don't who I am, I would like to learn and discuss how to live in Australia. I am worrying about you ignoring and misunderstanding me. I am still learning Australian culture, some things are very different so I am careful whatever I do right now. Especially with the English language.

Thanks for reading about my past life! And your help for my education.
Respectfully,
Nick.

What do you make of the situation now?
What advice would you give to Shirley after these further messages?
What do you think happened next?

PART 3

That was the final e-mail I ever received from Nick. I was still none the wiser. There was regret, certainly, but regret for having bared his soul to no avail, or for seeing that he may have unintentionally put me in a difficult position? The one comfort I drew was that although it was still clearly an emotional message, he really seemed to be closing the book on the situation: there seemed to be resignation in those last lines. I hoped that it had not taught him to be wary of people in Australia, that there was constant danger of misunderstanding.

Nick stayed away from my class for two weeks. For the rest of the semester I would smile at him in class, and pause beside him to give him the same help as I gave others. He never smiled back: in fact, he would never look me in the eye.

For me, it had been a frustrating experience that shook my confidence in my ability to empathize with students, to treat them with sensitivity, and give them appropriate language and learning support. I told my supervisor and the counsellor what had happened, and they were philosophical: all for the best, they said. For the student, clearly it had been a mostly unsatisfactory experience. Hope, of whatever kind, had been held out to him, and had then been taken away.

CASE REPORTER'S DISCUSSION

One of the challenging new aspects of student learning support – as indeed for all staff–student contact – is the fact that a growing amount of it is conducted via e-mail. Thus, relationships that were in former days more clear-cut, face to face encounters are now being negotiated by word alone. This means interactions are open to a number of hazards arising from the lack of face to face contact, not least of which is the potential problem of misunderstanding due to cultural difference. With the globalization of education, it is now possible that this will be compounded by students and lecturers being located in different countries. In those cases where there is little or no local support, the cultures of teacher and student may be remote from each other in every sense.

Early research into e-mail as a form of electronic communication suggests that e-mail is not, of itself, a 'genre' whose practitioners share understandings. As the mode of transmission is the only unifying feature, e-mail has a peculiar life, hovering – usually quite happily – between casual conversation and formal letter. Where circumstance (context) is not shared, there is potential for trouble. In this case, it is possible that the emotion of the student e-mail was released by the teacher showing him some individual attention: if the incident Nick quotes in his last e-mail is any guide, he was not used to teachers doing that in a positive way.

In the later e-mails, he did not seem to be embarrassed at having written like that in the first place; his concern was that the teacher had 'taken it the wrong way'. What was his purpose, in that first e-mail? He was clearly an unhappy young man, though not, seemingly, depressed: the e-mail is vivid and full of life. Perhaps he was simply reaching out, prompted by the expression of interest in his needs from someone who happened to be female. Were Nick and Shirley's respective frames of reference so different that miscommunication was always going to be a likelihood? Or was it simply that there was never the opportunity to develop common understanding about the situation? Arguably the student was, in fact, pouring out his heart, saying what he felt in all sincerity and with the simplest intentions. In this scenario, then, it was the teacher who did not write with total truthfulness. While as teachers we take pride in ourselves for developing close relationships with students, this tends to be on our own terms. We hold the position of power. This is a comfortable position to maintain, as evidenced by the discomfort we feel when we think we may be losing some control of the situation.

It is striking how the unfamiliar throws us. Given more time for reflection, before responding we may try to follow up avenues to find out more about, for example, the norms and customs of a student's country of origin. We may decide not to respond by e-mail.

CHAPTER 8

Dilemma for two

Case reporter: Eira Makepeace

Issues raised

The issue raised in this case is confidentiality in the context of a student bringing a dilemma to an adviser, the possible consequences of which are legal, ethical, academic regulatory, educational, psychological, and violence against the person.

Background

Mike was a geography student in the second year of his study. I am head of a student affairs department in an English university of 22,000 students. Most students seeking our help are referred to specialist services which provide counselling, financial assistance or careers guidance, but occasionally a student has unusual or sensitive difficulties and staff refer the student to me, as was the case with Mike.

PART 1

It was May, exam and hay fever time, and our Student Affairs department was tranquil. For me, though, it was not a tranquil time. Although my university has well developed student services and our department has a number of policies and procedures for dealing with students in crisis, there are always cases for which there is no procedure. This means we have to think our way through some principles before acting. These mainly concern confidentiality, which is always a thorny issue when the member of staff is an 'officer' of the university, the consequences of any action taken, the interests of the student and the interests of other parties. Sometimes these oppose each other and present the adviser with ethical dilemmas that can be of an unpleasant nature.

As head of the department, a member of academic staff and well experienced in student issues, staff tend to send me the most challenging cases. The situation with Mike was indeed an intriguing, disturbing and puzzling one.

On the day I met Mike, my secretary told me a male student at reception had a 'very serious problem' and she did not know what to do. This sometimes happens. Reception staff do not know in advance what sort of student problem will be presented and they can feel uncomfortable when listening to sensitive problems at the reception counter. And, despite their willingness, they may not always be aware of the intersection of some issues, such as our academic regulations in relation to plagiarism, or harassment of another student.

On this day, the receptionist ushered Mike in and, as per my normal procedure, we began by ascertaining details of name, year of study, address and other details. As casually as I can, I usually ask how the course is going and whether the student has done well so far.

Mike told his story slowly and tortuously. The essence was that he shared a university-managed house with two fellow students who had three non-university friends, and these 'friends' appeared to be crack dealers. He told me that one of the friends was a wanted criminal and sometimes stayed overnight. One night when the friends came round, Mike learnt that they had broken into a car and stolen a briefcase containing a passport, credit cards, laptop and floppy disks of a PhD student at our neighbouring university. He said that he could show me the passport, which at that time was in a kitchen drawer in the house. He had heard one 'friend' order items over the telephone using the stolen credit card. The house was under 'supervision' by the university since it was so dirty and because the housing office found out the friends were staying longer than overnight.

Although this was a somewhat unnerving case for me, we talked through some of his options. Mike was slight and short, and he was afraid that he would be hurt physically if he told the police. He said that he had already been threatened by one of the 'friends', who had stuck a sharp pencil close to his eye. Also, he did not want to worry his mother, so could not tell her, and he was worried about being an accessory to a crime.

He also said he had exams coming up. When Mike mentioned exams, flitting through my mind were the academic procedures in place for 'extenuating circumstances'. I knew that if the exam board agree to take the extenuating circumstances in mitigation, a student's overall grade may be improved and this can make the difference between passing or failing the year or the degree. Extenuating circumstances are many and varied but need to have seriously affected a student's exam performance when otherwise they would have been expected to pass. This may be death of a parent or close relative shortly before an exam, a serious car accident, acute illness, arrest, or theft of notes. Usually, things such as chronic illness, hayfever, quarrels with house-mates, or anything that occurred well before the exams, are excluded.

During my discussion with Mike, my extra-sensitive nose started to itch, and it was not hayfever! My nose usually plays up in the months before exam time in relation to particularly unusual cases. Often, the student's tale is accompanied by a request (usually at the end of the meeting) for a letter from me to the exam board to support the student's request for extenuating circumstances. But I do have to set aside the sceptical nose so that I can ascertain the legitimacy of the tale. If I discover in the discussion that the student has had poor marks throughout the year, my nose comes into prominence! What was the situation in Mike's case, though?

On hearing Mike's tale, I do not mind admitting that I was also afraid. What if I gave the wrong advice or became an accessory myself? Faced with this anxious student in front of me, what was I to do? Which of the issues and what principles should I consider first? And who could I turn to for guidance?

What do you think about Mike's situation?
What would you do if you were the student adviser?

PART 2

I heard Mike's tale through and discussed some of the options open to him. These were: tell the police directly or through an anonymous national line called Crimestoppers; move out of the house; tell his mother and/or tell his tutors. None of these found favour since in his view they all carried some risk. For my part, I was keen that Mike inform the police in an interview held away from his house so that the alleged robber would be caught and the personal documents reach their owner. However, I could also see a heavy-handed police raid on the house one night leading to an equally heavy later response against the only person who could have tipped off the police: Mike.

Mike then told me that he was also concerned about his forthcoming exams. My nose was feeling decidedly itchy as I asked him about his previous assessment performance and what grades he had received for his essays. He said that his marks hovered around 50 per cent to 60 per cent, which was adequate for passing. However, he said that he was now finding it difficult to concentrate on revision because of what he knew. He was worried because the exam mark constituted 75 per cent of the year's marks. 'How do you think I can help you?', I asked.

Mike wanted me to write to the chair of his exam board. In other words, he wanted a letter of his extenuating circumstances. I explained that if I did write such a letter, all it would contain would be the substance of his story and all I could say was how distressed he appeared. But I could not say any more than he himself could say since I had not a shred of evidence that his story was true. He then gave me the name of the person allegedly well known to the local police and said he would bring me some evidence the next day. He left my office, clutching a list of the options I had written out for him. He promised me that he would come back the next day and let me know his decision.

I considered my own concerns. Was I obliged to tell the police myself? What about the hapless PhD student whose stolen thesis and personal documents were allegedly in Mike's kitchen drawer? What about my colleagues in the university who had placed the house under a supervision order which was allegedly being breached? What about the safety of the other students in the house? What was my duty of care in these circumstances? What proof would I accept that Mike's story was true? Who could I turn to for some guidance?

My next step was to ring the university lawyer. I learnt that I had no legal obligation to inform the police, but if I was concerned, I could ring Crimestoppers myself. I would have to let Mike know I was going to do that, since I would be in breach of confidentiality. I could not be considered an accessory. I was also advised not to contact the other part of the university in charge of student housing since they might take action that could jeopardize Mike's safety. (I also wondered why they had not visited the house recently if it was 'under supervision', but knew that that was none of my immediate business.) I rang the local community police officer, told him Mike's story and mentioned the name of the alleged criminal. It turned out that he was indeed well known to the local force. I found that Mike could meet the police officer in my office and tell his story, without being identified.

I turned the questions over and over as I left for home. That night, I went to bed with a heavy heart.

I was both relieved and anxious at the same time when, next morning, I saw Mike waiting for me as I reached my office. He opened his bags on my desk and pulled out a passport, business cards matching the name in the passport, and a credit card with the same name. The name was not that of the students in the house (would they have printed business cards?) and I was closer to believing his tale than I had been before. My nose was feeling decidedly better! The issue of what either one of us was to do remained. Mike's issues were to do with his safety and getting a letter of extenuating circumstances. Mike had still not decided whether to talk to the police, still did not want to tell his mother, said he would be leaving the house after his exams, and would be going home soon, so moving out now was not an option and would not guarantee his safety anyway.

At this point I knew that I could, in good faith, draft a letter for him, but this was also something he could do himself. I advised him to write a letter to the chair of his exam board with a brief outline of his case and said I would add a covering letter. This would say that I had seen enough to convince me of his story and that if the story was indeed true, he would doubtless have had difficulty in revising and this could impair his exam performance. The idea was then to present it as a sealed letter, to be opened in case of academic failure. This meant that if he passed all his exams, the letter would not be opened, but destroyed. The letter had to be phrased sufficiently obliquely so as not to cause the exam board chair dilemmas similar to my own, but it could not be so oblique as to make the extenuating circumstances incomprehensible. I told Mike that if the letter was opened, it would be copied to all members of the board and be placed in his personal file. He had to think about that as well, since his file could be read in later years by staff unconnected with the exam board.

I told Mike about the police officer's offer of anonymity and he said he would think about it and get back to me. He would draft a letter, bring it to me and I would add the covering one. He would send both to his exam board chair. This duly happened the next day, and off Mike went with both letters.

So far, we had covered the extenuating circumstances. We had not addressed the issue of Mike's safety, and the theft of the thesis still troubled me. But without compromising Mike's safety, there was little further I could do. I was also left with the possibility that I had been suckered, but that was of little concern to me when set against my wider concern for the student's safety.

The story ended with a phone call from Mike's mother to say thank you for helping her son. I also made a phone call to the local police officer to say Mike would ring him if he felt he could. I was no wiser about the fate of the thesis or the credit cards and passport and certainly no wiser about the capture or otherwise of the known criminal. The following year, my secretary took a message from Mike to say he had passed his exams, and once or twice over the next couple of years he called by my office to say 'Hello', but I never happened to be there when he called. My secretary passed on messages of goodwill. I never knew for sure whether Mike's story was true.

Do you think that the appropriate action was taken?
What other actions could have been taken?

CASE REPORTER'S DISCUSSION

The most complex issues to do with managing students' difficulties usually have an ethical dimension. Sometimes ethical guidelines can help work out the best interventions for the student, but these also may not be the best interventions for others, including the university. In coming to the decision not to intervene by informing the police, I did not consider a set of rules or place these in a hierarchy, but followed a consequential perspective of trying to establish the goals I was trying to achieve, the means–end perspective. My goals, in order, were to ensure Mike's safety if I could, ensure he was well placed to pass his exams, try to rectify a harm done to someone else and, last, help effect the arrest of a criminal.

However, I had to realize that I could not achieve all these goals and still not pose a risk to Mike. I had to settle for attempting to ensure his safety, and that meant I could not blow any whistles nor help the PhD student who doubtless bitterly regretted the loss of his material. Equally, I had to put aside the fact that fraud was being committed and that the criminals would continue their practices. I also had to ignore the fact that other students of my university might be at risk. The questions I talked through with myself were along the lines of the good and harm I would do if I intervened, and the good and harm I could cause if I did not intervene. I came reluctantly to the conclusion that the best course of action for Mike was not to intervene in the matter of what had gone on in his house, but to stick to the academic issue at the heart of the matter: his need for a letter to confirm his extenuating circumstances.

The issue of confidentiality concerns any member of staff who has knowledge she or he would rather not have. The actual idea of confidentiality might seem relatively unproblematic, but in deciding a course of action resulting from the knowledge that is inherent in a secret, pitfalls abound. In other words, it is not so much keeping a secret, but knowing what to do with the facts of a secret that is problematic.

We also need to distinguish confidentiality from privacy or secrecy. In my department, we promise confidentiality unless we believe there is the potential for harm to come to the client or someone connected with the client in a particular context. In my case, harm could come if I breached confidentiality, not if I kept it.

Earwaker (1992) offers a five-dimensional model of confidentiality to assist decision making. The first is the level of sensitivity of the information. In Mike's case, the information was extremely sensitive and could not be disclosed. The second is the distinction between matters that are serious in their effects and those that are relatively trivial. Again, for Mike the reporting of his story to the police could have been potentially serious and could have jeopardized his continuance at the university had he been threatened physically in some way. The third concerns how far the information had a bearing on Mike's work. If his account was true, he would have found it difficult to turn in good work, and fear of the consequences would have adversely affected his studies. The fourth relates to the extent to which the student gives permission for information to be released. Without Mike's agreement, I was powerless to act other than to support his request for a letter. And the fifth and final concerns the variable of different levels of disclosure. I could have said 'my lips are sealed', a very strong form of secrecy. But I did not say this in case I later found I had a duty to disclose if I believed Mike was at risk of danger. I also had to be careful in not burdening academic colleagues with knowledge of Mike's case beyond that which would provide evidence of an extenuating circumstance.

So far, I have looked at the legal, ethical, regulatory and psychological aspects of this case affecting Mike and me as his adviser. But what had I learnt and what had Mike learnt from it all?

I had come to a rather sad conclusion common to many who advise students: sometimes, there is nothing to be done about a problem but to bear it. I had to live with knowledge that there were several wrongs I could have righted, but chose not to. Sometimes, no action turns out to be the best course of action. For Mike, despite the itches in my nose, he had learnt that someone in 'authority' had believed his story and had taken action to help him at a sticky time. Hopefully, he will have learnt to seek out others who can help him in his adult life, and if his visits back to my office are proof of that, he has learnt that even the most horrible problems can be helped.

I have never had a case like this before or since, but the requirement to manage complex dilemmas remains. The best advice I could give, and attempt to give myself, is to keep a cool head and an impartial mind and try to work out systematically what is in the best interests of the person in front of you. This may be best worked out after a meeting, not during it. Although I am fairly sure that it was not correct in Mike's case, an itchy nose is also useful when exams are looming! Above all, though, it is important to know that we may not be able to help solve all of a student's problems. Some will remain unsolved and unknown to anyone but the student and his professional confidante.

Reference

Earwaker, J (1992) *Helping and Supporting Students*, Society for Research into Higher Education/Open University Press, Buckingham

SECTION 2

DEVELOPING STUDENTS' ACADEMIC SKILLS

CHAPTER 9

I CAN ONLY DO IT WITH ASPIRIN

Case reporter: Linda Galligan

Issues raised

The main issue raised by this case is a mismatch between the view of a student learning support lecturer who wishes to develop a fundamental level of understanding in students, and the view that this is not necessary.

Background

The incident occurred in the early 1990s in a two-day workshop offered by an Australian university academic support department. Entitled 'Success in Maths for Nurses', the programme attracted about 60 of the 200 students entering the Bachelor of Nursing degree. The student cohort comprised school leavers, many of whom had not studied mathematics beyond a basic level, and mature aged students who had not studied mathematics for almost 20 years. The case reporter, one of the two lecturers involved, was about 35 years old at the time, with six years' previous high school teaching experience and three years as an academic support lecturer.

PART 1

A few years ago my son, who was then 10 years old, broke his arm while testing a home-made flying fox (a type of rope bridge) on the back verandah. We were very soon in the accident and emergency ward of the local hospital. My son, distressed with pain, was checked by the doctor, including being asked his weight, and then by a nurse, who asked the same question. After a few muffled discussions, some calculations on a scrap of paper (no calculator in sight), confirmation with a fellow nurse, and equipment being gathered, an amount of pain-killer was injected. Obviously, the calculations had been done correctly and his pain quickly subsided.

This incident clearly illustrated to me that nurses must have an overall understanding of the many mathematical, scientific and communication processes that are necessary in their profession.

Nursing educators address these issues as part of the curriculum. The best way of doing so, however, is unresolved. Most institutions that offer nursing degrees have a subject on drug calculations, and some also have mathematics support staff and support programmes. One support programme introduces students to some prerequisite mathematics skills, which also include scientific and communication processes, before they start their degree, and there are follow-up programmes, with or without support staff, throughout the degree.

But how do you get nursing students to attend a two-day mathematics workshop? At our institution, this particular workshop was taught *before* students started their degree, and after the school leavers had *had* three months away from school – a fairly cunning move! Students were sent a letter of invitation outlining the programme and, being as yet unfamiliar with 'typical university student' behaviour, were generally keen to come. The atmosphere was casual and students were introduced to some friendly nursing staff, as well as the two academic support lecturers and two tutors who were to teach the workshop. We also provided terrific morning teas. As far as possible, we were keen for students to do mathematics in the context of nursing. Hence, the materials were based around 'typical' nursing scenarios like: 'Suppose you are in this really poor part of the world with few resources, or let's say there has been a huge earthquake in the middle of Brisbane.' (Humour is useful in mathematics!)

Over the years of its operation, the workshop has been well received. While school leavers enjoy the workshop, it is the mature aged students who express their appreciation more explicitly. One typical mature aged person's response was, 'Should be compulsory for all nursing students who have not studied in recent years. It is a great chance to revise but also to meet and interact with fellow students.'

In the year that the incident described here occurred, the workshop was going smoothly, with students often breaking into groups to discuss problems or work on exercises. The first day was spent looking at four topics: routine observations (graphs); index of injury severity (fractions and tables); extent of burns (percentages and ratios); and measurement. Students generally required little encouragement to come for the second day (and not just for the morning tea!). Some recent school leavers who had achieved well in their final year asked if they could leave, as they were confident at this level of mathematics. On the other hand, some of these students actually stayed for the whole two days. As one student said, 'Even though I found most of the course easy, it was still good to brush up on my basic skills.'

On the second day we presented the topic of rates in the context of drug administration, which is always somewhat tricky to teach. Typically, you could teach it:

- by a formula; for example, dose required over dose in stock times unit volume;
- by the unitary method; for example, by taking it down to 1mL and then multiplying;
- by using equivalent ratios; for example, $\dfrac{10}{x} = \dfrac{4}{2}$ and then finding x; or

- by dimensional analysis (data entered as a single line of fractions in an ordered manner); for example,

$$\frac{mL}{dose} = \frac{16mL}{mL} \times \frac{1mL}{10000\ U} \times \frac{5000\ U}{dose}.$$

In fact, about nine different methods have been identified.

What we usually did was to show the students the first three methods and let them use the one with which they felt most comfortable, and that is what we did this time.

At this point, Ben, a student of about 19, became quite animated and somewhat upset. I had not really noticed Ben the day before and he had not said much. On the second day he was at the back of the room with a group of other students.

He suddenly piped up, 'Look! Aren't you wasting time teaching us all of this when all we needed to know is how to use those formulas?' He certainly got the attention of the whole class by that statement. He went on to say, quite assertively, 'All the hospitals have the formulas all over the place. My nursing mates don't have to worry about any of this maths stuff except when they have to do those stupid compulsory drug tests every couple of years. You know, those ones at the hospital.'

He was not aggressive or rude, but he was slouched in his chair waiting for an answer. I am not sure if he had a smug or a challenging look on his face. But as I looked around the room, I could see a few of the older students nod and many of the younger students looking towards me with interest.

What do you think the teacher should do?
What do think happened next?

PART 2

My first thought was, 'Great! Here is my chance to talk about mathematics and how it is part of everyday life; about its ability to help you think logically; about its…'. Luckily, I stopped myself. Obviously, if he had been engaged over the last few days, he would have realized my position already. I still thought it was a great opportunity to talk about a very important issue. During the development of the workshops, I had the experience of talking on this issue to practising nurses as well as the nursing staff at the university. Some of the mature aged students in the class had been working in hospitals or nursing homes, and I decided to use them as a part of a strategy. I noticed Joan, one of the older students, nod as she listened to Ben, and as we had already had more than a day of group and whole class discussion, I felt comfortable asking Joan her opinion.

'Is this your experience as well, Joan?' I asked her.

'Well, yes and no,' she said, and then added, 'I'm not allowed to give out drugs or any of that stuff, but I do notice nurses just follow the instructions given. There isn't much maths at all. Most of the time it seems pretty straight-forward, but there are some times they have to check everything is correct, like the drip and that, but then I don't work in intensive care or paediatrics.'

A couple of other experienced people had similar opinions to Joan, and most had noticed the charts that Ben had mentioned. One of the students who had long experience with drug administration said, 'I can do this type of… well, maths, I suppose. I can do it easily, without thinking, like with aspirin and stuff, but you ask me about those other chlorophenolblah blah things and I have no idea. Yeah, I can only do it with aspirin!' Everyone laughed at that.

I did not want the discussion to continue for too much longer, so I said something like, 'Ben, if you want, you can just do these problems using the formulae, and Janice,' I said jokingly, 'you just think of aspirin, but I'll show the class the other methods and they can choose which method they like.'

Could anything else have been done to convince the class of the usefulness of the approach?
Would you have responded differently?

CASE REPORTER'S DISCUSSION

As academic support staff, we constantly see students who are unsure of and unfamiliar with the necessary mathematics skills; some are maths phobic; and some, like Ben, see little necessity in studying beyond memorizing a few formulae to get the right answer. They have varying degrees of confidence and widely different ages, experience and learning style. Hopefully, we can give some of them confidence and skills in mathematics, relieve them of some of their maths anxieties, and we can even give people like Ben a broader view of mathematics. But it is difficult to do all of this. We find it difficult to cope with the differing demands of the students, the demands of the faculty staff to 'fix them up', and the educational philosophy, which is often at odds with the pragmatic solutions available.

The issue of the best method to teach drug calculations to nursing students highlights this pragmatic versus philosophical approach. This is occurring against a backdrop of the changing nature of mathematics support, where it should no longer be seen in isolation from other academic support. Indeed, in many institutions, it is moving towards an integrated approach with faculties aiming to improve university teaching and learning. While this is a positive move, it may pose a dilemma for the academic learning support staff.

One such dilemma is the teaching of rules to do drug calculations. In the typical medical calculations course, there are sections on different types of drug delivery; oral (tablets and liquid), injections and intravenous drips. From an expert point of view, these all use the same concept (rate), but for a novice, they are often seen as separate. With each type of delivery, there is a different formula and a different set of rules. It is relatively easy to teach students each rule for each delivery type and ask them to sit a straightforward rule-based test, and they usually pass the test. Students are happy – they have passed. Nursing staff are happy – the pass rate is high. The problem is that students come across the problem again in a year's time and many have forgotten how to do it. And what if they come across a problem that does not quite fit the pattern? What method do they have to fall back on?

It turned out that Ben had a fairly good grasp of mathematics and found quite a few of the sessions easy. In a way he probably could not see the mathematics in the situations I was presenting. As one student said during a taped interview I conducted a few years later, 'It's just simple stuff, not mathematics.' Other students struggled with many topics introduced in the course and found each session very helpful.

So what should I have done about Ben? A 'formula' method is a useful tool for students, but it should only be part of a nurse's 'mathematical toolbox' to be used as the need arises. Ben's mathematical toolbox was well stocked and he did not recognize that he was using other tools. I could see that he was not simply applying a formula. When the need arose, he would convert units, multiply a dose by the weight of the patient, then apply the formula. He also understood the formula. But other students could not see this. By arguing with Ben at this stage, I would not only have alienated Ben, but made other students feel inadequate that they could not do it Ben's way. By allowing Ben and the others to select the method they felt most comfortable with, I was then able to summarize during the session about how the different methods were similar, and that students should choose the one in which they were confident. I now also have a small collection of nursing anecdotes which demonstrate the diversity of approaches that nurses take in doing drug calculations. I also tell them the story of my son's broken arm.

From my experience in teaching mathematics, and more specifically drug calculations, to nurses, I have noticed that students do have different preferences for learning and have different difficulties. Some students fear fractions; some dislike division; often students say they do not understand decimals, and many are apprehensive about metric conversions; some students do not like using calculators and others cannot perform the operations without them. Many specifically say, 'I prefer to use formulae; I prefer to use ratios; or I just like to think about it.' In nursing practice there is even more diversity. Pozzi and his colleagues (1998) found that some nurses used different methods, depending on the drug itself.

Should we encourage them to use the formula method because it is the method used in the hospitals, and what some nurses use? Do we ask them to memorize the formulae? Should we encourage a dimensional analysis because it has a neatness of set-up? Should an introductory course attempt to introduce many different methods that may just confuse students? While one student said in her evaluation, 'Helped me to understand, not just accept the formulae', another student said, 'You should ensure that your method coincides with those used by the pharmacology and toxicology lecturers.' There is no simple answer to this conundrum for the academic support staff, but it will depend on the relationship between the academic support and the nursing staff.

Reflecting on the course now and the incident with Ben, I think there are wider issues to consider: teaching and learning issues as well as a broader issue of transfer of knowledge and understandings.

Teaching in this support area does not take place in isolation. The role of the nursing staff is crucial to the success of the nursing workshop. In subsequent years, I have asked a nursing staff member to attend at the beginning of each session and say why *each* session was important. This has had a very positive effect on the workshop, and students have often written in their evaluations about the helpfulness of this interaction. Because academic support staff are generally not experts in the field of nursing, the presence of an expert reinforced and endorsed what I was teaching. This included the importance of thinking beyond the formula. From both their experience with teaching nursing students and communicating with nursing staff, the academic support staff teaching the workshop now have an awareness of many of the broader nursing issues. They often address the drug formula issue before it arises, asking the question that Ben put to the class. It is surprising how often students will put forward counter-arguments similar to my own.

Understanding student learning is critical, in terms of not only what they learn but how they learn. The issue that Ben raised is important, and one with which the support staff (and the nursing staff teaching the drug calculations) at all nursing institutions around the world have to deal. Throughout the degree, it is emphasized that patients do die from incorrect dosage administration. One of the major problems is that much of the process of delivering drugs is now more automatic as the drugs are pre-delivered in the correct unit dosage. Nurses no longer routinely perform many calculations (except in intensive care and paediatrics), and when the calculation is not automatic, it is difficult for nurses to remember what to do. We must use our expertise as academic support staff to facilitate this recall. Routine learning of formulae is a useful tool; even now I can easily recall part of the formula, 'dose required over dose in stock'. But to assist students in their learning, we must help them become aware of, reflect on, transfer and improve use of their mathematical tools.

A final, broader issue for academic support staff also arises from the case. This nursing workshop is but one example of the mathematics support we are expected to provide for the university community. There are many similar programmes that we may support, for example, statistics, economics or physics. What worries me is that we are busy producing mathematics in-context programmes which students clearly like, but such programmes may make the student dependent on the expert to do the transfer for them. Once the in-context mathematics programme allows the student to make sense of the mathematics, the next step is for curriculum designers to develop students' knowledge and competence throughout their degree studies. But in doing so, they must also develop students' metacognitive, metacompetence and transfer abilities. In such appropriate designs, academic support staff as well as the subject lecturers have a role to play in assisting students. The challenge is to determine the best way to achieve this.

Reference

Pozzi, S, Noss, R and Hoyles, C (1998) Tools in practice, mathematics in use, *Educational Studies in Mathematics*, **36**, pp 105–22

CHAPTER 10

ACCOUNTING? I CAN DO THAT

Case reporter: Linda Forson

Issues raised

The issue in this case study is that of helping first-year accounting students to survive their course in the context of a very high failure rate.

Background

Vista University is a multi-campus, historically disadvantaged, black institution of higher education in South Africa. This case study takes place on the Welkom Campus, which is in the goldfields mining area of the Free State province. Despite being a mining community, many students come from rural towns and from severely deprived educational environments. At the Welkom Campus, students' examination results have been notoriously poor. In 1996, for instance, there was a 94 per cent failure rate for first-year accounting students.

PART 1

A six per cent pass rate for a higher education course is unacceptable anywhere. This is particularly so at an institution aiming to assist students to become leaders in fields such as management sciences where, because of past apartheid policies, there is a critical shortage of black graduates. What exactly was the problem? Was it simply that the schooling the students had received before beginning the course was inadequate, or was the university failing students through poor teaching, support, motivation or selection? Everyone was very concerned about it.

Staff in the Department of Student Development were grappling with the problem and discussed it extensively with staff in the Department of Accounting. One suggestion was to introduce a foundation programme to help students develop the skills underpinning their studies before they began. But there seemed to be little support for this from some areas. In fact, the dean of the faculty at that time commented, 'If they can't make it at first-year level, they shouldn't be at university.' This view dismayed us, as it was expressed in the context of the self-fulfilling attitude that black people could not work with figures. In turn, we knew the effect was that black students came to believe that they could not succeed in areas like mathematics and accounting and they avoided these fields.

Those who were more aware of the situation knew that this was not the whole problem. It seemed that under-qualified school teachers of subjects such as accounting were not preparing students adequately, thus leaving gaps in their knowledge. This made it very difficult for students who wanted to study accounting or conceptually hierarchical subjects such as mathematics. Where gaps exist in knowledge and understanding in such a subject, it is important to provide first-year university students with a broad but thorough introduction to the basic concepts needed for success. But whose responsibility was it to provide this instruction? While the complexity of the problem was recognized by the new dean, and while academics debated possible models to address the problem at departmental and senate level, the students on campus needed help.

Finally, a wave of action was activated to address the problem. Academic staff were fed up with the poor pass rates of students and approached Mr Jadrijevich, Head of the Department of Student Development, for help (this Welkom Campus initiative spread later to only two of the other seven campuses). Mr. Jadrijevich and I as the learning adviser were the staff assigned to address the issue. We were keen to help the students and enthusiastic about taking on the issue, but we were also a little scared. We had to decide where to start – how best to try to improve the situation. It was a big task, and we knew we would face problems, but we were committed to developing the best response that we could.

What do you think are the main factors they need to take into account? What do you think they should do?

PART 2

Mr Jadrijevich and I met and considered the alternatives. Finally, we settled on an approach. As we were both enthusiastic about developing a general

Supplemental Instruction (SI) programme, we decided to investigate the possibility of adapting SI for Accounting.

From our previous work, we knew that SI aims to assist students to gain the necessary skills to succeed in courses that are generally considered difficult, through peer assisted and voluntary sessions. We knew that, traditionally, black students work together and study in groups, even if it means 'overnighting', which is the practice of studying right through the night for a few days or a week before an exam, individually, or more often in groups. Peer assistance is appealing in a culture where black students are painfully shy about asking for information or addressing staff on any issue. 'I don't think we'll have any problems with this approach,' Mr Jadrijevich commented to me. We both believed that having senior students facilitating learning through group learning techniques, and often in the vernacular spoken by the group, would improve the students' success rate. Our role in the Student Development Department was pivotal to the success of the programme. We would set up the programme, provide training, and facilitate and monitor the programme as it developed.

Through the discussions with our accounting colleagues, we decided that the SI programme would have to be adapted to allow for maximum practice of problems, rather than for understanding theories. We knew that our students were not used to spending two to three hours working out problems as a means of mastering techniques of application. We hoped that regular attendance at SI sessions would compensate for gaps in many students' knowledge because of their non-attendance at mainstream classes. As many students had not taken accounting at school level, discussing concepts and terms during SI sessions was meant to fill in gaps. We limited the groups to a maximum of 10 students. Hopefully, this would encourage students to talk to each other and to the leader, to develop interpersonal communication so that the isolation of being new in a strange environment would be minimized. Immersing our students in the regularity of relatively 'open-ended' sessions would, we thought, provide a model.

Another factor that we considered was the relative freedom of first-year university life. It was commonly thought that female students especially did not cope well with their new-found freedom, and that this contributed to high failure rates. Students often attend sessions regularly in the first semester, but attendance declines in the second term as they begin to enjoy the freedom of university where no one checks their attendance. Female students become involved in relationships and drop out of studies, or lose interest in achieving as relationships become more serious. However, our experience was that in the SI class, female students attended regularly.

Unofficially, we called the accounting programme ACC-I-CAN, because it had a positive motivational ring to it. Officially, it was called the Accounting Potentiality Development project, reflecting our view that students have the potential to succeed in accounting, but that it needs to be developed and reinforced.

How does it work? In our programme, we had the extremely important role to play of gaining the cooperation of lecturing staff who would provide worksheets containing example problems based on the planned lectures. The SI leaders, for whom we provided regular training on aspects such as communicating clearly and logically, recognizing and responding to students' learning difficulties and managing groups, work through the problems themselves and discuss with each other students' potential difficulties. During weekly facilitated sessions, the students work on problems individually or in small groups. The SI leader guides students towards the correct answer through questioning and suggestions. We included this aspect in the programme to engage students actively in the learning process and to model good study practice.

Although we never expected it to be easy, we faced very severe obstacles. The first was finding sponsorship for the programme in order to pay for senior students' involvement and so on. The second was recruiting and training senior students. The third was marketing the programme extensively, and the final obstacle was avoiding academic staff 'dumping' the problem in our laps.

After we had been running the accounting SI programme for some time, we tried to get some idea of how students responded to the programme. That is, how much, if at all, was the programme of benefit to them in their accounting studies?

The first question we asked was if the programme helped students in their study of accounting, and in what ways. Some of the responses were as follows:

> Yes, it has helped me and it is still helping me because I pass the modules. I haven't done accounting at school but it seems as if I have done it because I pass it. The sessions are very helpful to me.

Clearly for this student, the SI programme has been able to compensate for a lack of background study in accounting.

> Yes, because we were given extra exercises to practise and that has helped me understand the course even better.

This student is pinpointing the need to practise exercises and reinforce principles in applying them to problems posed in accounting.

> Yes, it has helped me because since I attended I have improved my marks and even my attitude towards accounting, and I do understand the work more, than attending lecture time.

Despite poor grammatical use of English, this student is reflecting on her changed attitude towards the subject and her perceived improvement in conceptual understanding of the work. She highlights the problem experienced by many students, that attending lectures on its own is not enough and that the students have to practise or grapple with the problems. She also implies the usefulness of students forming study groups or having tutorials in which problems can be teased out.

In response to the question of what students think they need from the university in order to become employable, they responded:

> I need to have skills from my lecturers in order to qualify for a job and practice is very important – that means to practise what I will be.

> It will be better if the university can provide us with some service in order to get working experience or provide some post for students or organize some companies to give students practical training in order to get experience.

> The university must provide us with good in-service training in order to get experience eg getting to big companies like Anglogold to do articles as volunteers and be granted certificates.

Clearly, the students appreciated the programme. It gave them practice in accounting skills, and improved their confidence and motivation to study accounting. The failure rate, although still too high, declined from 93.68 per cent in 1996 to 45 per cent in 2000. The failure rate for our campus was also much lower than that for other campuses, and we concluded that the SI programme has, at the very least, done no harm!

But the students' comments also indicated to us that they were very concerned about entering the workplace, and that English language skills would need some assistance. We could help with the written English by building skills into our programme; however, the work aspect was more difficult to tackle. Perhaps our next move would be to consider building work experience into the syllabus for the SI programme, or even putting forward the idea of a foundation programme. We are still thinking about that one!

What do you think of the outcome?
What can you learn from this case for your own practice?

CASE REPORTER'S DISCUSSION

Clearly, action had to be taken quickly and the Supplemental Instruction approach was one with which both Mr Jadrijevich and I felt comfortable. We also knew that it had been successful in other settings. On the Welkom Campus, the focus is to integrate study skills, literacy and writing skills into mainstream activities. The SI programme is exactly such an attempt. In the process, accounting practitioners and academic staff feel very strongly that students should become independent learners, taking responsibility for their studies as soon as possible. As a result of the legacy of apartheid, most students at the campus come from educationally disadvantaged backgrounds and are used to rote learning and poor teaching.

The SI in the ACC-I-CAN programme took an interactive approach, encouraging students to develop their independence by working in groups to solve the practical accounting problems, rather than relying solely on their teachers. The major advantage of this approach is that it encourages cooperation and collaboration among students, breaking the isolation that they often experience. A further advantage is that students gain experience in teamwork, in working with others to arrive at a solution to the problem at hand. In so doing, they need to be able to assert themselves within the group, as well as cope with other students who may be too assertive! We feel that this is very valuable experience that serves a purpose in addition to assisting students to pass accounting; the skills can be transferred to the workplace, where teamwork is highly valued.

A disadvantage of this approach is that, in university study, students are expected to be independent learners. How can the two be reconciled? Student performance is measured at an individual level through examinations and tests, and there is no provision for group assessment. From student results, a pattern can be seen where individual students who score high marks from the beginning of the year maintain this standard throughout. Our experience is that group work seems to reinforce their potential, but we would like to do further research on the ways in which it assists students.

Another underpinning principle of the SI programme is that students practise examples. The most significant benefit arising from this is that it can assist to fill gaps in students' knowledge. As an area emerges where particular students are having difficulty, other background factors can be explained. Furthermore, students who did not have accounting as a school subject have the opportunity to catch up and practise techniques and applications. As students are completing the problems, they become skilled in these tasks, and, importantly, can pass the exams. It can be argued that practice without theoretical background may lead to a rote learning approach. Will this assist students to be able to apply skills to new situations they may face in the workplace? Perhaps the best approach is to combine the theoretical explanation with the practice.

In communicating with their SI leaders, students are able to use their vernacular language. Through working in their first language, students feel more comfortable and are therefore more inclined to express their difficulties and gain resolution to their problems. Students find it difficult to express their thoughts and ideas clearly through the medium of English. A way to combine the benefits of the use of the vernacular with experience in English is to encourage students to take the English for Business Communication course that is also offered. Students who do this are at an advantage when it comes to the more formal written and oral communication involved in their studies. Perhaps this should be made compulsory for students, as barely five per cent of students enrolled on the campus have English as a first language; for the majority it is a second or third language.

Here, we need to emphasize that we are aware that in the university students are expected to use a more formal style of English, especially in their written assessment. Furthermore, they will be expected to use this in the workplace. Another suggestion would be to include written English instruction alongside vernacular language in the classes and to explain to students the different settings in which different forms of English are suitable. Politically, encouraging standard or even academic English has been a thorny issue, based on educational or global arguments within an emerging African nationalism. The institution needs to give clear guidance with regards to language policy.

Some staff believed that black students were not competent in subjects such as accounting. It is important that this conception changes so that it does not become even more of a self-fulfilling prophecy. But will the SI programme assist in changing attitudes? The main way in which the SI can assist here is that, the more students pass the examinations, the more it provides concrete evidence that students have the potential to complete their degree programmes, provided they have initial support. This negates the attitude that black students cannot work with figures. As students gain confidence after positive experiences in their first year, they generally continue to pass second and third year, thus increasing the number of graduates as well. The fact that students who did not have accounting at school level pass first year debunks the myth that they are not suited to accounting. Students also recognize the need to develop skills they do not currently have, in order to succeed in the workplace. Such awareness points to a level of perception and intelligence with which staff have not always credited students. It is clear that in most cases, the students are determined to make the most of their time at the institution and gain a rounded education. As one student put it, he wants to become 'a sophisticated person'.

A problem, however, is that students place very high expectations on tertiary education and the SI programme. Although the programme can stimulate students to take responsibility for self-actualization, the programme cannot address all ambitions that students may have for their future lives. There are also difficulties for staff steeped in a Western tradition that values working individually, which may be outside the life experience of students in the African context. Clashes may even occur where a student has to make a decision to succeed within a Western model; this may contradict with his or her African culture.

Academic staff can be more involved in the programme. Of the two major advantages of teaching staff involvement, the first is that students see the staff as interested in them and their learning. This motivates students and gives them the encouragement needed to approach staff. Currently, very few students overcome the cultural barriers in approaching senior staff.

The second advantage is that teaching staff can inform the programme more directly regarding the types of cognitive skills and competencies they wish their students to have achieved by the end of the year. However, teaching staff may want the SI leaders to do more than their time allows or the SI programme has planned to achieve. As the purpose of the programme is to improve learning and successful retention of students, teaching inputs are highly valued.

Overall, the SI programme is successful in addressing the immediate problem of pass rates. The original pass rate for the Welkom Campus in 1996 has improved dramatically in 2000. Comparing the results in terms of pass rates between the seven campuses for the period 1996 to 2000, it is clear that the Welkom Campus pass rate grew steadily and was maintained.

The significance of this pass rate is that it means more first-year students pass into second year and therefore, theoretically, spend one year less in completing their degrees because of not having to repeat a year. It also serves the purpose of raising questions and issues including critical thinking and assessment, which otherwise might not come to the fore. As the programme starts afresh in a new year, the concerns and issues raised must be incorporated into the training of new SI leaders and discussions with faculty or teaching staff. But as with many support programmes for student learning, the perennial question that comes to mind is where support ends and mollycoddling begins.

CHAPTER 11

WHAT'S INFORMATION LITERACY?

Case reporters: Dolene Rossi and Leone Hinton

Issues raised

The issue raised in this case concerns assisting new students to develop information literacy skills as they make the transition to higher education.

Background

The students in this case were undertaking a common core course 'Health and Community' for higher education programmes in nursing, occupational health and safety and health promotion. The School of Nursing of an Australian university offered the subject both nationally and internationally, utilizing internal campus-based and external distance modes of teaching, across regional campuses. The consequence was a student cohort diverse in context, location and culture.

PART 1

The teaching team was under pressure. We had an attrition rate of 33 per cent, despite the inordinate amount of time we were spending supporting our students, on top of our increasing workloads. We understood that our students were in their first year and that many were new to higher education, so we were making a concentrated effort to assist them in understanding the academic requirements of the course as well as introduce them to our subject. With little success!

The course 'Health and Community' focused upon introducing and describing the concepts of health and the factors which impact upon it, such as history, politics, health systems, socio-economics, communities, culture and ethics. The topic was central to the programmes and the professions chosen by the students. Yet we were finding that more and more of our time both inside and outside of class was being spent assisting students to access information, draw comparisons between different sources and highlight the relevance of different information in different situations. We expected our students to be able to select appropriate health information, for specific client groups, in a variety of health contexts. We assumed that the information would come from a range of credible sources including texts, journals and the Internet. In reality, we were presented with articles from *Woman's Weekly* magazine and quotations from *Encarta*. It was evident that the students were collecting information in a random, non-discerning fashion, which was reflected in the quality and type of information contained within their assignments.

We could not understand it. All students participate in an orientation week just prior to the start of the term, and one of their first visits is invariably to the library. In their mentored groups they meet the faculty librarian, are shown the resources available to them and listen to their mentor stressing the importance of understanding how the library functions and where and what to find in order to complete assignments. Weren't they listening?

The limit of our endurance had been reached. It was during a team meeting that the point of no return arrived and we agreed that we had had enough. Jenny expressed the sentiments of us all in stating, 'I don't know how long we can continue to support these students in this way.' Clearly, the students needed to know how to access and manage the information themselves. We could not keep doing it for them. We urgently needed a new approach.

What do you think we should do?
Where do you think we should start?

PART 2

We began from what we knew about our students, recognizing that they came from diverse backgrounds, were varied in age and ethnicity, had different learning styles and had selected either an internal or external mode of teaching. Could we capitalize on these factors rather than see them as obstacles?

Above all, it was apparent that we should 'work smarter, not harder'. We brainstormed our aims and objectives for the course and what we hoped the students would achieve by the end of the 12 weeks. Our expectations were high. We wanted students to gain knowledge of the subject area and an understanding of how the various concepts impacted upon the health of both the individual and the community. Underpinning this was their ability to find and use in appropriate ways information from a range of sources. Through the teaching and learning process we hoped the students would develop academic skills which would be transferable across courses, contexts and establish a foundation for lifelong learning.

We examined our interactions with the students because, in the interests of equity, we wanted to provide both internal and external students with the same information and resources. We discussed our ideas with the faculty librarian, a previously under-utilized resource whom we had consulted in order to improve course content and for personal research activities. Our consultation confirmed and legitimized the skills we hoped to develop in our students. She introduced us to the term 'information literacy', and it became increasingly apparent that the students were not the only ones with a lot to learn. As a team we recognized the personal challenge ahead. We were excited at the prospect of doing something different, but the real driving force was the idea that we would free up some of our current student consultation time.

So what did we mean by information literacy and what skills did we expect our students to develop? The roles of information searcher, information user, technology user and organizer epitomized those required. It became clear to us that these roles would become functional as the students developed information literacy skills. We expected the students to develop the ability to recognize the need for information, and the technological skills that would enable them to access that information from appropriate sources. We envisaged them being able to analyse critically and evaluate the information they obtained and use it effectively in a decision making process. We expected them to be aware of the potential ethical, legal and socio-political aspects of information and the technologies. We anticipated their ability to generate and effectively communicate information and knowledge and, finally, we hoped they would develop an appreciation of the relevance of lifelong learning.

Although a little awe-inspiring, our research suggested we were not the first to consider these valid information literacy competencies and that the State University of New York had already developed material that could inform our own teaching and learning process (SUNY, 1997).

Given our aims and objectives, we needed creative solutions in order to deliver and teach information literacy to students across a wide geographical area. We also wanted students to recognize that these skills could be applied across programmes, contexts and cultures and throughout life.

How could we best set about using the knowledge we had gained?
How could we integrate course content and information literacy?
How could we assess both subject knowledge and information literacy skills within the course?

PART 3

Our conclusion was that the key to integrating information literacy skills with the content of the course was through the teaching approach adopted and the form of assessment tasks we selected. We also felt that the success of the endeavour, in terms of skill transfer and lifelong learning, would be determined by the extent to which students recognized the value and application of the principles to other courses and real life experience.

We chose to adopt a modelling approach to learning experiences. In this way we could imitate reality, be active, cater for a wide range of learning styles, be up to date and develop a non-threatening learning environment. Although it was confronting and a little disconcerting at first for many of us, we used the approach predominantly in lectures and tutorials. Within the session we introduced a health-related concept and one of the information literacy skills (for example, culture and search strategies), illustrated how each of these applied to the various disciplines, and demonstrated through the literacy competencies the application in relation to the course assessments. To assist in the learning process we also used a narrative story-telling style and role-modelled accessing, assessing and evaluating information using computers and the library training room. Initially, several team members argued that this approach would take too much time away from the content aspect of the subject. But as we linked information literacy with the subject content, it became feasible to integrate the skills in this way.

We developed three assessment pieces for the course which were consistent for both internal and external students, with some adaptation required for students with geographical constraints. The assessment tasks used the subject content of the course as a medium through which students were able to demonstrate their acquired information literacy skills, apply them to situations that reflected their personal backgrounds, and consider their application to situations other than their own. The tasks were developmental and designed to reflect the progression of the student from an individual with personal life experience, to the student as a health professional and the student as a scholar. This corresponded to and facilitated the progressive development of information literacy skills over the 12-week course.

Initially, students were required to identify and search for relevant information, from a variety of appropriate sources, for a specific health-related purpose, thereby meeting the roles of information searcher, information user and technology user. For the second assignment, they had to provide some justification of the relevance of information included in the first assignment. This made it necessary for students to demonstrate their ability to critically analyse and evaluate information and apply effective and creative decision making skills. The third and final assessment required the student to submit a paper, similar to those submitted for journal publication. In effect, students were required to utilize and demonstrate the full gamut of information literacy skills required to function well within the university environment and within their chosen profession.

The outcomes of the course were identified explicitly. We introduced the redesigned course the following term during orientation week. As a part of the course, an introductory session to Health and Community for all internal students was conducted, and video conferencing technology was used to ensure that the information provided to students was consistent across campuses. For those studying at a distance, this message was conveyed both in writing and on video-tape, and we established a group teleconference early in the semester to ensure students had access to the teaching team. We also encouraged the use of e-mail and creative voicemails in order to provide access to relevant information.

In order to avoid potential difficulties with our distributed campuses, each teaching team of lecturers and a librarian advisor were given resource based teaching kits for the redesigned lectures and tutorials. The kits included content information, the information literacy skills to be modelled, and discussion topics that related to the scholarly work required in various health contexts. Throughout the course we continually referred to the relevance of the subject and information literacy to other courses within the programme, providing examples and real life experiences.

Overall, our approach has been received positively. The appreciation of the students, specifically in relation to the application of the information literacy skills in the real world, has been reported and documented through repeated qualitative course evaluations. Initially, verbal reports from the coordinators of other courses within the students' programmes suggested that the information literacy skills developed within 'Health and Community' were being utilized across a range of subjects. This anecdotal evidence was later supported by course evaluations designed to determine the extent to which students applied these skills across their programme. Since the restructure of the course, students have continued to utilize the search strategies and information competencies developed in their first year to address assignments throughout their second and third year of higher education.

What do you think of the outcome?
Can you identify a practical application of our approach in your own work?
Can you think of any ways to improve the approach adopted?

CASE REPORTERS' DISCUSSION

Upon completion of the course, we reflected upon those aspects we considered successful and those that were not. It was apparent to us that the sequential nature of our process, in both the teaching environment and the assessment items, was highly successful, and students responded positively to this in their evaluation. They were also appreciative of the fact that we worked hard at making the connection to the world of work and specifically to their disciplines. To our delight and relief, the information literacy competencies were seen to be transferable to other courses and students reported these skills as being beneficial to them.

However, there were several flaws in our approach, from the students' perspective. We had placed an important emphasis on the basic use of information technology, assuming that students would be able to turn on a computer and access the Internet. In reality, we found that there were students who did not have the skills or equipment required to do this. As a result, they needed extra tuition, which they sought from local libraries, from the off-campus librarian or from children and friends who had some knowledge of information technology.

We discovered that our expectations relating to the students' ability to critically analyse and evaluate the information and then apply this in a decision making process were a little ambitious. In fact, we found that the students' knowledge and experience in these areas was so limited that they had difficulty discerning the relevance of the information and its potential application in their assignments. And for some, the problem was more fundamental in that they struggled to understand the content of what they were reading because of the specialized language used. However, we felt with more practice and exposure through other courses, these skills would be developed over time. We did believe it was important to continue to introduce these skills in conjunction with the other information literacy competencies within the context of the course.

A more basic conceptual problem in relation to the course subject became apparent through the assignment submissions, particularly the scholarly paper. Although some very good papers were produced, students were still bound to the stereotypical aspects of health – more particularly those perpetuated by television shows like *ER* and *All Saints*. These biomedical media portrayals of health issues present the students with a very one-sided view of health, and this impinges on how students respond to thinking more broadly about the concepts this subject has to offer. Their almost blind adherence to the supremacy of the view presented in the television shows interferes with their ability to evaluate the credibility and contribution of information from a range of sources. Somehow, we have to address this issue and assist students to see that the media portrayal is only one way of perceiving a medical situation, and to debunk these preconceived viewpoints. We will have to do this through our presentation of the content and information literacy skills of evaluation of sources.

From a teaching perspective, we consider ourselves to have been fairly innovative, pooling our resources, working as a team, incorporating methodologies which were both flexible and challenging. Personally and individually, we had to 'let go' of the relative safety and comfort of 'talk and chalk' and live the learning experience. And innovative practice comes with a price, a price that some lecturers are reluctant to pay. In our case, our commitment was rewarded with both professional and personal development.

Recognition of the value of our redesigned course by our colleagues within each of the programmes has lent support to its continued integration in the curriculum. The restructuring process required us to have or develop a sound knowledge of curriculum development and the teaching–learning nexus. Our personal training needs analyses highlighted deficits in our knowledge of electronic sources, of the socio-political, ethical and legal aspects of information literacy, as well as the need to increase our proficiency in using search engines. In effect, the process of restructuring also served to inform and advance our own pursuit of lifelong learning. So the project, which started out as a means of reducing student contact time, did in fact result in a journey of discovery for both students and staff.

The critical issues raised in this case concerned how new students can be helped to develop the information skills required to make the transition to higher education. Can first-year students develop information literacy skills in conjunction with subject content, and effectively apply these skills within the duration of a course? And are such skills transferable across courses, contexts and cultures? The evaluation of our course has consistently demonstrated positive outcomes in the area of defining, locating, selecting, organizing, evaluating and presenting information relevant to the health concepts explored. However, it is the firm belief of the staff involved in teaching this course that the actual result transcended these outcomes and involved what is described by Yerbury and Kirk (1990: 23) as, 'the development of personal or transferable knowledge and skills, self-confidence and self-awareness, initiative, autonomy and commitment to action'.

Acknowledgements

We would like to acknowledge the work of the teaching team in Health and Community: Mrs Margie Wallin (librarian extraordinaire), Mrs Sue McIntosh, Ms Jennifer Jones, Ms Jenny Klotz, Ms Trish Robins, Ms Sansnee Jirojwong and those students who have contributed to the development of this subject and the model by which it now operates. Thank you.

References

State University of New York (SUNY) Council of Library Directors (1997) SUNY CLD *Information Literacy Initiative: Final report* [Online] http://olis.sysadm. suny.edu/ili/final.htm

Yerbury, H and Kirk, J (1990) Questions of professional practice: innovation in the education of information professionals, in *The Changing Face of Professional Education*, ed M Bezzina and J Butcher, AARE, Sydney

CHAPTER 12

HOW CAN WE REACH THEM?

Case reporters: Esther Daborn and Bill Guariento

Issues raised

This case study looks at how language and academic support for both home and overseas students can be integrated into an undergraduate engineering course where teaching is by lab and lecture.

Background

The events described here took place at the University of Glasgow in Scotland. They involved collaboration between the Electronic and Electrical Engineering (EEE) Department and the English as a Foreign Language (EFL) Unit on a third-year course with an average class size of 110 students, half of whom are home students and half from overseas.

PART 1

Five years ago our EFL Unit was feeling elated. We had been asked to assess third-year undergraduate EEE report writing, and identify students who needed English Language classes. 'Great!' we thought. 'A chance to assist with "writing across the curriculum".' However, our jubilation was tempered when we realized that, following the traditional style of the EEE Department, our input for the EEE students was to be a one-hour lecture on report writing in term one. Thankfully, we could give guidance on 'goals' by including criteria for assessment, but there was no chance to let students see a model, or to practise the process.

The essence of the mismatch between our own and the EEE Department's approach was that in our unit the approach was very student-centred. We subscribe to the view that the process of learning to write is cyclical. Students do an assignment, receive feedback, and try again next time. This means they are told *what* to do and then receive feedback on *how* they did. To supplement this approach, we have a flexible range of delivery: from formal to informal, personal to electronic.

'Still,' we thought, 'at least with a lecture our work is integrated and it is better than dealing with students on a one to one basis.' So the lecture went ahead. And when the reports came in we followed up with a thorough assessment programme. This involved six EFL tutors marking 110 scripts and giving individual written feedback. We then set up three levels of support, based on the 'classical' distribution of the results: a handout for the top 25 per cent, a handout and three hours of classes for the mid 50 per cent, and 12 hours of classes for the bottom 25 per cent.

There was no doubt about the support that we could expect from the EEE Department. They were right behind us and assisted us where they could. However, the timetabling of classes was a nightmare. We were also very worried about some home students whose first language was not English. In our view, they needed at least 12 hours of language support. Furthermore, their language problems were different from those of students who had come from overseas. An inharmonious mix was created when home students found themselves in the same class as students from overseas. As is our normal practice, we evaluated the programme at the end of the set of classes. The higher scoring home students showed either that they did not need the help because they knew it already, which was fine, or that it was useful. There was no follow up from either the EEE Department or from the EFL Unit on this or other assignments in terms two and three. The problem was left dangling.

We have repeated the same lecture input and assessment procedure over the last three years. We have not been surprised to learn that the EEE staff still think that there is something wrong with their students' writing. In discussion with them, it is clear that they think it might be to do with clauses and commas. For a while, we thought that the way to improve the situation would be to hold staff workshops on guiding and assessing student writing, but the department declined our offer. Our suggestion that it might be a good idea to talk to students was also met with a negative response. There seemed to be a belief that the EFL Unit should *tell* the students *what* to do. We had reached a stalemate.

This year, however, heralded a change of direction. The impetus for this was that the EEE external examiner made adverse comments about student communication skills. It resulted in a new course called Career Skills 3, which is a much broader-based communication programme which includes assignments on report writing, CVs, a business letter, and a technical essay. Unfortunately, our input is still the same one-hour lecture. We offered again to give staff workshops, only to be met with horror. No time! Staff are heavily committed to research.

What were we to do? We could continue to make our 'token' effort, but we knew that results would be limited. Our commitment was to facilitating learning. How could we respond?

What would you do in this situation? What would be your approach? What do you think actually happened?

PART 2

An answer came to the rescue that seemed very obvious once we had thought of it. This was an electronic and electrical engineering department, so what could be more appropriate than utilizing the computer and the Web? Here is a mode of delivery that is flexible enough to circumvent lectures, unread handouts, timetabling problems and unhappy class mixes. Fortunately, we were not starting from scratch. We had already produced some online materials for writing humanities essays, called 'Outlines'. Their broad learning goal was to give a general feel for the genre. They take the student through the general process of working out what a title means and, through links, they guide the student to make use of the instruction words, context and grammar in order to select a suitable pattern of argument for their essay. We offer five types: Listing, Compare and Contrast, Cause and Effect, For and Against, and Situation–Problem–Response–Evaluation. Each argument pattern is linked to a template for creating a logically ordered outline. At each stage there are samples, and for each pattern we have created a model outline and essay. So far, so good. We thought we could adapt these to include EEE essay titles.

But our talks with the EEE students clearly indicated that the mix of students meant that there was a wide range of language problems. Consequently, the 'Outlines' materials were pitched too high. They assumed knowledge of academic style and the meta-language of grammar. By contrast, EEE students tend to write as they speak; they have a limited idea of what makes academic discourse special and a relatively rocky grammatical base, which means a patchy understanding of the difference between, for instance, a verb and an adjective.

We talked to EEE staff and realized that there was too much navigational freedom in the existing materials. Having assumed that students had a certain amount of academic baggage, the structure of the materials meant that students could choose the order in which they would read the pages. Aghast at this, staff in the EEE Department were adamant that their students needed to be presented with the material in a far more predictable way.

So it was back to the drawing board for us. A major rethink was required in terms of content design, especially the simplification of stages in the essay planning process, and expansion of the type of language support to cover academic style conventions as well as basic grammar points. We started by breaking down the process into three basic stages: analysing the title, gathering information, and organizing information.

A key change in 'analysing the title' was to narrow the learning goal to an approach in which only one essay title was analysed. We called this 'unpacking', and added the use of different colours to identify instruction words, key aspects, and significant information. The EEE students needed to view the title in a more basic way, as a portal to a fairly prescribed essay template, similar to the process of setting out the design template of an electrical circuit. We were drawing on what they knew and understood to create a bridge into the writing aspect of their studies.

For 'gathering information' we placed the focus on time management, amount of information (complete with a likely word count), and the need to record accurate bibliographical details along the way.

For the final stage in the planning process, 'organizing the information', our initial idea was to use an authentic and impressive mind-map produced by one of our (more proficient) students, showing the 'process' from reading plan → detailed notes → writing plan → first draft → essay. But two problems surfaced here. The first was technical. Scanned pages of the 'scrawl' that typifies all brainstorming and notes (whether good or bad!) become virtually illegible on the computer screen. The second problem involved content, because our proficient student was studying education. The EEE tutor threw up his hands in horror at this. The EEE students would not be able to adapt this model to their own subject.

Here was another impasse, which was finally solved by the tutor giving us a sample essay called 'What is the future for electric and hybrid electric vehicles?' We pounced on the model. There was no lack of essay titles, but we did not possess the content know-how needed to write models, as we had done in the 'Outline' materials. For the 'organizing information' section we created notes extrapolated from the essay and showed the process of harvesting main points, and fitting them into a logically ordered outline.

So much for the planning process. We have said that, in view of the linguistic weaknesses of the EEE students, we aimed to present this in a fairly regimented manner. However, we did allow for an element of flexibility when it came to expanding language support by making a frequently asked questions (FAQs) section, catering to students both stronger and weaker than the EEE norm. The FAQs covered academic style conventions as well as basic grammar points. Depending upon their level, students might choose to learn by looking at models, or to use our Web pages as an online grammar resource.

For students wanting to see a model of style and structure, we had only one at our disposal, and we have exploited it thoroughly. From the FAQs page we linked to separate sections to demonstrate introductions, conclusions, citing sources, bibliography, paragraphing, and tense use. In fact, the need to use this one essay as our model throughout has been, perversely, a strength, because it gives the student who lacks confidence a safe point of reference.

For students needing to use the FAQs as an online grammar resource, we set up a choice to suit different problems. A simple problem might be a question of punctuation or sentence structure. For the more ambitious students there was a link to a deeper level, a more sophisticated look at 'writing powerful sentences' and a section on 'how can I give my opinion?' At a more detailed level we still provided links to pages outwith our material, for example a dictionary, detailed grammar site and exhaustive list of commonly misused words.

As a final safety measure to cover any problems arising, we set up an e-mail box at the foot of the FAQs, so that any student with further questions could contact one of our EFL staff. (See 'Writing a Technical Essay' at http://www.efl.arts.gla.ac.uk/Links.htm#writing)

CASE REPORTERS' DISCUSSION

The challenge described in this case was to come up with something that would suit home and overseas students, and could be integrated into the curriculum without impinging unduly on student or staff time. The online solution caters for a mix of levels, and avoids timetabling problems. The response has been positive. From informal discussions with quite a number of the EEE staff, we know that they like the materials because they are wide-ranging. They deal with a wide range of issues to do with writing, from commas to how to give an opinion. The students like them because they are simple and logical, thus easy to use. We have invited comment from learning support staff in other disciplines. They like the layout and think that the content design is consistent and well thought through. They want to adapt them for use in other subjects.

We think there are several reasons why these online materials work. The first is that the opportunity to meet the students and talk to them gave us a 'feel' for our audience. Students cannot always articulate their problems, so there is a fair amount of interpretation involved at this stage. Also, we have taught essay preparation courses for many years in different formats according to need. We know what it means to take students through the 'how'.

The second is the fact that we were able to get a passable model essay. The EEE course director understood what we were doing and helped to make it work. The third is the fact that we were able to offer a mix of guidance using a 'process' approach, models, and access to rules. The EEE students feel comfortable with the prescriptive nature of the process, and the choice of logical argument patterns; it has an affinity with being told a lab procedure.

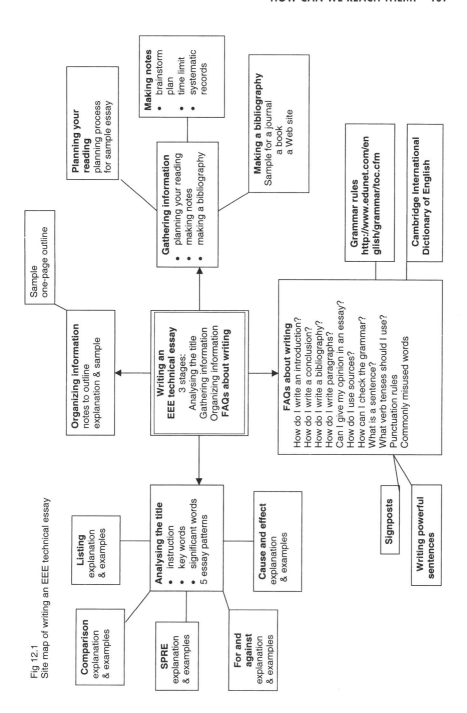

Fig 12.1
Site map of writing an EEE technical essay

They are being given a template. They know what to say; they want help with the 'vehicle' for conveying the message.

'Aha!' you might say. 'What do you do about technical expertise?' The answer is that you gather it yourself: very slowly. We have developed expertise from teaching with online materials, observing how students learn, and understanding the features of task design in this mode. We have looked at a large number of sites and observed style characteristics to make sure we could maintain user-friendliness. We made the decision to eschew the complexity of interactive tasks because you have to second guess students' answers. Instead, we offer reference and personal communication via the e-mail box. This is the nearest we can get to a tutorial.

For technical matters, time is important. The work took about five weeks, including designing, writing and testing the Web pages. It involved two members of staff, of whom one was keen to learn html. We also had access to technical support for the tricky bits. This was the third set of online materials we had worked on, so we already knew some of the pitfalls such as poor navigation.

Of course, this online solution does not fully address the problem. Can we reach all of the students who need help? Those who make use of support are usually the bright ones wanting to do better. And let us not forget the cyclical nature of writing development. We have not dealt with the assessment and formative feedback aspects.

The next question is, 'Does it work for the students?' They have not handed in their essays yet. Watch this space!

CHAPTER 13

READING FOR LIFE

Case reporters: Faridah Pawan and Sharon Pugh

Issues raised

The case is concerned with supporting ESL and other under-prepared readers in higher education so that they can acquire confidence, flexibility, and strategic approaches to reading and learning from texts.

Background

The case involves a Korean graduate student admitted to a demanding MBA programme in a large American university. Like many international students, he was in need of English language support and had been referred to the Intensive English Programme (IEP). He had not had extensive academic reading and writing experiences in his native language. Of the two instructors, Faridah has been a lead IEP instructor for several years with ESL/EFL students at all levels of English proficiency. Sharon has been director of the campus's academic support unit for many years, with experience with second language speakers and extensive knowledge of strategies for under-prepared learners and readers struggling with academic literacy skills.

PART 1

We met Jae Hyun in the advanced reading classes in the IEP where we quickly noticed he showed signs of depression. What he told us of his state of mind confirmed this observation. How could things be going so badly for him in the United States, he was thinking? He told us that he was elated when he was accepted into the MBA programme at our large university. It was a prestigious programme and Jae Hyun had no doubt that he was on the threshold of unlimited opportunity. But now, after more than a year, he was still struggling to keep up with his reading assignments. On top of this, he had been asked to continue to take English classes along with his business studies. He had already taken all of the ESL courses in the programme, and many of them twice. 'How can this be?' he asked himself many times a day. 'Do I really belong here?'

Yet we knew that Jae Hyun was an exceptionally bright, responsible and dedicated student and had a lot of experience that was relevant to his studies. Before arriving in the US, he had started his own computer consulting business after working in two corporations. This experience along with his previous college record gained him unqualified acceptance into the competitive graduate programme. But here he was now, very frustrated and even more embarrassed by his difficulties with academic reading in English. His confidence was at such a low ebb that he doubted whether any language programme could help him. As a last measure, he had made inquiries about hiring a professional reader and note-taker, an expense he could ill afford.

This combination of academic ability and reading difficulty was not, in our experience, unique. Many students like Jae Hyun stay in the Intensive English Programme for a year or more, taking the same classes, often several times. After gaining acceptance to their desired programmes, they find themselves stuck in a kind of English limbo, some being advised to keep repeating courses, others lacking the confidence to go into their regular studies, all paying high costs in time and money for delayed progress toward their primary academic goals.

We had to try something different. Conventional reading and study skills approaches did not seem to be working with Jae Hyun and those like him. Often students failed to make a connection between such skills instruction and their immediate reading needs. Our first idea, therefore, was to increase authenticity. We had students bring texts from academic courses they were taking or provided texts from our own collection representing a variety of disciplines. We hoped that making a direct connection between their English and their academic learning would help increase students' sense of purpose and motivation in our classes. 'Besides, if we watch what they do with their texts,' Faridah suggested, 'we might also be able to informally diagnose their specific difficulties.' Sharon agreed.

When we sat down with Jae Hyun and his business management text, however, we were surprised by the level of anxiety he exhibited. We knew he lacked confidence, but we did not expect him literally to freeze with the book still closed in front of him. Without even opening it, he said he knew it was too difficult. 'How do you know when you haven't tried?' we asked. He lowered his head in painful embarrassment, and for a moment we were afraid he might even cry.

'I have tried,' he said in a low voice. 'I read the first three chapters, and I can't remember anything in any of them, or even the main points they were making.'

Thinking he would do better with material for which he had some background knowledge, we chose a chapter on small business ownership, but that did not help. It was as if he had never thought about this topic. He read laboriously, trying to extract every bit of information from the chapter as if his own knowledge had no relevance to what he was learning. After a couple of pages, he could not discuss anything he had read.

How could we assist Jae Hyun to overcome his fear of reading and lack of confidence with academic texts?
How could we help him to engage actively with texts rather than merely extracting information?
What do you think will happen next?

PART 2

We came together to discuss strategies. Although Jae Hyun was the immediate concern, we were interested in developing an approach that could generalize to other students. Our complementary backgrounds working with ESL, EFL and the general population of under-prepared college students proved useful as we devised a new approach. We settled on a three-pronged strategic plan that would cover a period of eight weeks: first, help students overcome their negative attitudes toward reading or themselves as readers; second, provide them with concrete strategies for effective reading; and third, address the issue of meaningful engagement with texts as well as their own authority as writers.

As a beginning, we planned to take students on several visits to the local public library. Its friendly, civic-oriented environment contrasts with that of the often intimidating, ten-storey university library, the sixth largest in the nation. With its comfortable furniture, social areas, and colourful displays of magazines, videos, CDs and tapes, the downtown library provided the perfect atmosphere to warm students up to reading and melt their frozen attitudes toward print.

After a chance to explore the library on their own, students would then be invited to choose their own reading materials while we instructors joined in, enthusiastically searching out books we had been wanting to read. Not everyone immediately picked up on our enthusiasm. Coming from highly structured academic environments, we could see that many were uneasy with this loosely structured, seemingly non-academic experience. Jae Hyun, who wanted quick strategies that would help him transfer the contents of texts to his memory, showed frustration with our neglect of what he termed as 'real and serious' reading. Although he and the others went along, it was clear for some time that they had difficulty seeing how browsing in a local library related to their immediate concerns about their courses.

At first students' choices of reading material were mainly newspapers and magazines. But by the end of the first week, many were also choosing books, often following our example by seeking titles they were curious about such as *The Catcher in the Rye* and *To Kill a Mockingbird*, or novels on which movies had been based, such as *Dangerous Minds* and *Seven Years in Tibet*. We all confessed to never taking the time to read for pleasure, and many seemed genuinely pleased that this class was going to afford them a chance to do so. In this approach, which emphasized personal experience with texts, we felt that it was important to let each student find his or her own material with which to engage.

The first novel Jae Hyun chose was Umberto Eco's *The Name of the Rose*, with which he did not get very far. This experience initially increased his frustration with himself as a reader, so we helped him find another novel, *The Joy Luck Club* by Amy Tan, which might relate more to his own intercultural experiences. We were thrilled to see that as he read the novel, the immigrant experiences of the characters in *The Joy Luck Club* resonated so strongly with his own experiences that he began naturally to transact with the text, as if he could not keep his background knowledge out of his reading. We also observed him 'bookmarking' especially significant parts of the text, which formed a structure for remembering and reflecting. At this stage, we were giving similar support to every student, helping each make the connection between the active, exploratory reading we were encouraging and learning in an American university.

With Jae Hyun, it was important to help him acknowledge his true reading level and devise a strategic plan to move beyond it. For example, he was extremely dictionary-bound at first but was embarrassed by his dependence, often apologizing when we 'caught' him looking up a word. Rather than either encouraging or discouraging dictionary dependence, we taught him and other students to create their own dictionaries of words they did not understand, putting in them their own hypotheses of word meanings as they derived them from context and constantly tested them in further readings. Jae Hyun enjoyed this process and used his dictionary to good advantage. It helped him to move away from a dependency on external sources and use contextual information as well as his own knowledge and reading experiences.

After two weeks of reading independently, we asked students to select a novel to read together, and they voted for Jae Hyun's choice. Now we were ready to move into the second stage, teaching specific reading strategies. We formed reading circles of three students, each of whom had a specific role to play. One was to summarize for the class what the group felt was most significant in that day's readings, another was to suggest themes and issues emerging from the reading, and the third was to relate the issue to something outside the text, which could be another reading, a film, or an experience shared by the group members. To support students in these tasks, we taught skills for summarizing, extracting themes and arguments, and finding linkages between texts and other sources of knowledge. We also showed video clips of the movie version of the novel, brought in a storyteller who told a story with a similar theme, and entertained a panel who discussed the experiences of first and second generation Asian-Americans. Our purpose was not just to spice up the sessions but to show students how any given text is always part of a much larger web of meaningful sources.

Finally, we had students respond to *The Joy Luck Club* in both academic and creative ways. As an academic activity, they researched and composed a 5 to 10-page paper on an issue emerging from their discussion of the book. Despite their initial view of themselves as virtually non-readers in English, they were able to follow through on their own inquiries quite successfully. In addition, they wrote stories that reflected their personal and emotional responses to their reading. To support them in this endeavour, we provided a Web site (http://php.indiana.edu/ fpawan/welcome.html) (which still works!) which guided them through steps in plot construction and gave them tips on character development. Jae Hyun, in particular, put his heart into his story and revealed a side of himself we had not seen. He wrote a pseudo-biography of himself and invited readers to choose one of three possible endings: one, the main character reinvents himself in another career; two, he gives up the whole quest and dies in infamy; and three, he finds inspiration to continue the quest in the form of a female companion.

To pull things together, we ended the session by reviewing with students all the activities we had undertaken, the strategies we had tried, and how they related to academic reading. We talked about how important students' own knowledge and interests were in the learning process. Then we drew parallels between what they did with the novels – discussing, analysing, sharing issues and ideas, and following up with inquiry and writing – and what they should do with academic texts. Finally, we discussed how important it was for students to regard themselves as readers and to welcome all kinds of opportunities to engage with texts. We praised their participation and products in the activities and described how we saw their growth as literate learners.

We cannot claim we worked a miracle with Jae Hyun, but we did observe a definite change in his attitude and self-confidence right away. The work he put into his projects was evidence that he was taking control of his learning and experiencing a sense of success. He began immediately to apply his new strategic approaches to reading in his business classes and, just as importantly, overcame his embarrassment enough to approach his professors for guidance. The following session, he remained in our programme but taking only one class, and he made good use of other campus resources such as the Writing Tutorial Services and the Student Academic Center. The semester after that, he left the nest completely but has joined a reading circle for post IEP students. We sometimes see him on campus, looking sharp in the suit that is the uniform for MBA students, and he is confident of achieving his academic goal.

CASE REPORTERS' DISCUSSION

This case illustrates the possibilities for opening students' minds as readers so they can make full use of all their resources as learners. It addresses the issue of overcoming barriers of fear and frustration for second-language readers and, by implication, all reluctant or inexperienced readers. We first addressed this explicitly by taking students to a library with an inviting and friendly atmosphere. Our approach then led students into new territory as readers, encouraging them to use their own knowledge and experience to make sense of texts so that reading becomes an active, engaged process rather than the labour of transferring text into memory. It also combined critical creative thinking, in the analysis and discussion as well as in the inquiry projects that are part of the approach, and creative thinking, by encouraging personal interaction with self-selected imaginative works which illustrate alternative ways of dealing with themes and issues. There is also a possible release of intellectual energy previously held hostage to self-defeating beliefs about one's reading abilities and the nature of reading to learn.

Obviously the great challenge in this approach is to break through the common mindset that reading is absorbing the information and ideas in the text without reference to one's own knowledge and perspectives (Chi, 1995). Some students may never let down this barrier, especially not in a short session. Others may participate, but not as fully as Jae Hyun, because they cannot easily give up their reserve, they remain relatively passive readers, or they do not find a book that facilitates their aesthetic reading as *The Joy Luck Club* did Jae Hyun's. Before he found that novel, he became even more discouraged by trying to read one for which he had no background knowledge or intrinsic interest. There may also be an element of bibliotherapy in this approach (Cohen, 1992) in that literature can be a vehicle for students to understand and deal with issues in their own lives.

We also noted that at the beginning Jae Hyun was still intent on extracting information from his novel, engaging in what Rosenblatt (1978) would term as 'efferent' reading, namely reading to mine for information, rather than 'aesthetic' reading, which involves reading on creative and critical as well as literal levels. Aesthetic reading calls for the interplay of reader and text, what Rosenblatt calls 'transaction'. But Jae Hyun had initially lacked the confidence to put his own experience and ideas alongside the authority of his English academic texts. His identification with the characters and the events in *The Joy Luck Club* in a way forced him beyond the level of superficial reading. In essence, Jae Hyun took ownership of the reading and took charge of his own comprehension of its contents, and this, we tried to reinforce for him, was what he should do in all his reading.

In our deconstruction of our first experience with this approach, we spent much time considering second-language issues and general reading issues. We saw them as very interrelated but acknowledged that students may not see it that way. As second-language readers, students were especially concerned about their lack of vocabulary and were constantly interrupting their reading to look up individual words. While we did not want to encourage students to go through the motions of reading when they really did not understand, we also wanted to give them a greater sense of control in this area and a way to organize and retain the vocabulary they were learning as they read. Hence, we had them construct their own dictionaries, which would allow them to keep adding to the meanings they were developing as they encountered terms across texts. This approach also set them up to acquire academic literacy in their fields, since learning specialized terminology is essential to mastering any discipline.

We had seen the rigidity with which many students approached academic texts as a problem for many American as well as international students. Fostering greater flexibility and personal ownership of reading was crucial in helping students become the eclectic, adaptable readers they would need to be for success in demanding academic programmes. They had to be convinced that there are no short-cuts in reading to learn. It is either an involved, multi-faceted experience in which knowledge accumulates across texts, across courses, and across disciplines, or it is simply the efferent, information-specific reading which may be adequate in highly technical situations, such as following instructions or learning specific systems, but falls short of any situation where ideas and dialectical thinking are required.

Jae Hyun, along with the other students, needed to feel that the reading class helped him undertake academic challenges. Working on a research paper helped meet this need, along with exercises demonstrating the interrelatedness of reading, writing, and research, the three pillars of academic literacy at the university level. At the same time, creative experiences helped show that reading and writing can serve less obvious purposes by opening channels to new ideas and ways of thinking through issues, even reaching into previously inaccessible areas of thought.

There are many logistical issues in this approach. We were lucky to have an excellent local library within walking distance of the campus, but not every situation is so fortunate. An alternative is to build up a classroom collection of imaginative as well as academic texts and keep adding to it as new interests are brought to the fore. This requires funding from some source, often the teacher's own pocket, which sets obvious limitations on it as a strategy. One may need to visit the book sections of second-hand shops and thrift stores, solicit donations of books from colleagues and students, or have students themselves find other sources of reading. This approach is also very labour-intensive for the instructor. Not only does one have to provide a major source of collective energy in the early stages of the programme, but one has to spend a lot of time guiding each student. We found our own collaboration an enormously important part of the experience. We could put our heads together on all issues, from individual student needs to planning a week's activities, and we depended upon each other for all kinds of support in everything we did. Carrying out this approach alone would be very demanding, though not impossible.

In the end, with all its challenges, we are committed to this approach and the basic principles upon which it is based: that all reading experiences are useful in new situations, that the reader's knowledge, reasoning, and imaginative thinking are all valuable resources not to be ignored when encountering new material, and that reading that addresses the emotional needs of students while it provides the means for developing intellectual/academic skills has almost incalculable value. This value will be apparent, however, only when students feel they are acquiring the specific strategies they need to succeed in their major programmes. So we must keep showing them how they are developing effective reading skills that they can transfer across situations and languages.

References

Chi, F M (1995) *Discussion as Inquiry in ESL/EFL Reading: A study of Taiwanese college students' meaning-construction of a literary text through small group discussion*, paper presented at the Annual Meeting of the Teachers of English to Speakers of Other Languages

Cohen, L J (1992) *Bibliotherapy: The experience of therapeutic reading from the perspective of the adult reader*, Michigan University Press, Ann Arbor, Michigan

Rosenblatt, L (1978) *The Reader, the Text, the Poem: The transactional theory of the literary work*, Southern Illinois University Press, Carbondale, Ill.

CHAPTER 14

Back on course – but...

Case reporter: Vanessa Charter

Issues raised

This case raises the issue of a university student with dyslexia.

Background

Geri was a second-year student taking a degree in communication and media in an institution in the UK. Struggling with her work, Geri eventually sought advice from her local Dyslexia Association. The case is reported by the dyslexia consultant whom Geri approached.

PART 1

One Monday morning an urgent voice called me from my desk to listen to a mumbled message left on our help line answer machine. A distressed and sobbing female seemed to be in desperate need of help. It was so difficult to decipher the call that it took three of us to re-listen and retrieve the caller's name, Geri, and number. While it is not uncommon to receive this type of call, it is always disturbing. By chance I wrote the number down and so it was presumed that I would return the call.

I took a long, deep breath and phoned Geri. A first call is often difficult. Usually there is a need for the caller to 'unload', which can be lengthy and somewhat circuitous, ending up where you started out and with no resolution. My introduction was calm, stating my name and that I was returning her call. I was therefore a little shocked, because Geri was not sobbing, but pretty aggressive.

'Why,' demanded Geri, 'after sailing through early schooling as a bright pupil, have I failed my second-year final examinations and had my last three assignments returned for resubmission?' I remained silent and she continued with some admissions. Geri was honest enough to admit an erratic work record, some attitude problems and feeling depressed. I detected an angry and very disappointed student. But I was reminded of the sobbing desperation of her phone call and gently enquired if she was dyslexic. She did not know, but a fellow student had suggested this, and so we began the process of Geri being taken on as my client. I arranged a dyslexia screening consultation for the next day, assessing this as a priority case, wary of Geri's mood swings and the prevalence of depression and suicidal thoughts harboured by some adults with unidentified dyslexia.

At this stage, I naively thought that all Geri needed was a dyslexia screening test and to take the result back to the university, where she would receive a full dyslexia assessment and access learning support. How wrong I was! The screening revealed that Geri was likely to have a specific learning difficulty such as dyslexia, and I recommended a full educational psychological assessment. During the consultation Geri revealed tell-tale signs from earlier difficulties at school, sixth form college and university. For example, concentration was difficult, timekeeping was poor and personal and study organization were problematic. There was even talk of bullying from peers and sarcasm from staff. Geri's school reports revealed a plethora of 'could do better' remarks and comments about careless spelling, attitude and application. I explained that dyslexia had only been officially recognized by the government in the last few years. But here we had an able student showing signs of *underachieving* and no investigation was in process. I telephoned her university, which was sympathetic, but refused to fund a dyslexia assessment for Geri (which is expensive) because of her failure to reach the criteria for returning for her third and final year. My heart sank and I began to feel I had bitten off more than I could chew. We are always short-staffed and I had no free time.

When I explained all this to Geri, she crumbled, fighting back tears and revealing she was in a complete mess at university, with her studying and with her life. She described her experience of asking her English tutor if she might be dyslexic and was told 'No', and to 'Get down to some work'. After my phone call to the university, I realized that this was a fair comment considering Geri's attitude, her tardiness in handing in assignments and that the staff received no dyslexia awareness training. But Geri was beginning to worry me because there were other issues, such as heavy drinking binges and sleeping problems. I was beginning to find myself in deep water and decided to ask her what the university suggested before she returned home. Geri explained that learning support was in the process of initiating a new department and looking into staff appointments (as with many establishments). And so, continued Geri, it was left to her tutor to tell her that she must resit her examinations and resubmit three essays before the end of August, now only 10 weeks away! Just what was it that Geri was wanting from me? 'This is a ridiculous situation,' I thought to myself.

What sort of help do you think Geri needs if she is to return and succeed? What is the consultant's role, what is the university's role?

PART 2

Common sense told me that it is impossible for a failed student to complete three essays and study for exams in such a short time. Besides, even if Geri had a dyslexia assessment it would take at least three weeks to receive the results. Then the university needed to find a specialist dyslexia tutor who could support Geri with her mountain of work, by which time only six or seven weeks would remain. No, somehow I had to explain to Geri that it was all too much and too late. I began by asking Geri what she really wanted, but she was not sure, she could not understand what had gone wrong and added that she wished she had worked harder. Carefully and quietly, I asked her if she wanted to leave university. Her mood changed and she retorted with a fiery, 'No, but they will throw me out anyway.' Talking to Geri was a rollercoaster ride, her moods were changeable and I was careful about broaching issues.

On the other hand she liked her subject. Schoolwork and examinations had not presented problems before and she had good qualifications. Geri was a typical bright and able student with possible unidentified dyslexia, which would not be considered a problem at school. Yet now I was facing a young student who was on a downward and dangerous path of educational failure and self-harm. I searched for the right words but found it very difficult to decide how to advise Geri. Instead of suggesting she leave university, I heard myself saying that unidentified dyslexia affected adults quite severely and that she needed to know whether or not she was dyslexic. Then, and only then, was she to decide what to do. In the meantime we could look over her essays and work out a timetable for her exam revision.

What was I saying? In the back of my mind I realized that there was no funding for this assessment, but decided to appeal to the trustees to fund the bulk if Geri could fund at least some of it. All agreed, and an assessment was booked for the following week. I must have been mad, I had no free appointments, had never supported a student in higher education and felt as if I was drowning. Something about the misfortune of Geri's situation reminded me of my long journey towards recognizing my own dyslexia. I reminded myself that I was becoming personally involved and to proceed with caution.

The educational psychologist identified mild dyslexia with moderate attention deficit syndrome, explaining many of Geri's difficulties and, in particular, her lack of concentration and mood swings. Geri's mild spelling difficulty was in visual perception and visual sequential memory. Sequencing problems affect sentence order, planning work, time (starting and finishing) and reading comprehension (expending energy decoding text rather than comprehending makes reading laborious). At last Geri had some explanations, and was pleased to note she had a high IQ (128) and deserved to be at university. For a short while, we sat in my office laughing over coffee and a celebratory doughnut. The euphoria was short lived; nothing had really changed and I still had some deciding to do.

If you were the dyslexia consultant, what would you do next?

PART 3

Geri's assessment results vindicated any doubts I might have had about my decision to support her. I made up my mind to give up some of my holiday time to help Geri if she chose to attempt resits: it would be an all or nothing campaign. We decided to contact the university with Geri's results and try to work in unison with them. Unsure quite what I was taking on, I felt that all parties should attempt to work together and apportion no blame. The university was helpful and I managed to speak to Geri's tutor to discuss whether the offer to return still stood. It did, but the university required Geri to prove that she was committed by resubmitting three essays before the beginning of term and resitting two of the four exams. If successful, Geri would receive advice from the learning support department for her final year.

There and then, somewhat fired up by the sequence of events, we worked out a timetable for study support and homework. Bearing in mind Geri's attitude to work, poor planning and organizational problems, I helped her draw up a humorous, coloured timetable with enough time to watch television or listen to music daily and socialize once a week. I reminded her that drinking a couple of litres of water daily would hydrate her brain, increase concentration and aid memory. We had fun learning the rules of mind mapping, stimulating all the senses with colours, pictures and scented felt pens. I took in some building blocks (concrete material) to represent sentence structure, topic sentences and paragraphs. We practised SQ3R (Cottrell, 1999), to access academic text and to select relevant chunks to revise.

Geri needed to know that there were many more ways to learn. I referred to dyslexia affecting her learning and how to use her strengths such as thinking in pictures, three-dimensional thinking, good long-term memory and verbal skills to support her weak areas. Reading by visualizing text increases comprehension by 40 per cent, creating models in the mind aided by self-talking for revision or planning. Gradually, Geri learnt that dyslexia is a different way of thinking and that she could 'upskill' in her weak areas by using her strengths.

Teaching intelligent dyslexic students through their preferred learning styles is revealing. Geri was a concrete processor (needing plenty of examples and demonstrations) with a random ordering style (needing help with organization, time and structure). However, this concrete random style tends to create some spectacular critical insight and intuitive observation. Geri's typical dyslexic profile synthesizes material by linking information and ideas together that are unusual, insightful and innovative.

Armed with new skills, Geri began a daily plod through her timetable and rewriting the essays proved to be easier than she expected. As with many dyslexics, the content of her essays was sound, but the order, sentence construction and general structure were confused. Any marker might be forgiven for not understanding how a bright, articulate student could produce such poor work. Sadly, the effort expended in the piece handed in rarely represents ability.

I gave up two hours per week for four weeks, and three hours for each of the final two weeks, to help Geri restructure her essays and revise for her examinations. At times I wondered if it was worth it or if this was an impossible task. Was what we were attempting possible?

Actually it was. Geri discovered that it only needed a reorganizing of sentences, paragraphs and a bit of restructuring to rewrite her essays – and one was awarded an A-grade! In fact, Geri did not rewrite her essays but restructured them, with some help in proofreading for meaning, as many sentences were reversed (out of order). Geri returned to university in the autumn, graduated with a 2:2 honours and secured well-paid work. The story had a happy ending.

Or did it? About a year later I invited Geri to join my 'learning styles and dyslexic adults' research, only to discover it was not enough to identify dyslexia, teach a few study skills and scrape through a degree. Issues about what it means *to be dyslexic* concern issues of identity. When I caught up with Geri, she was unhappy and failing *again* and had pre-empted being sacked by handing in her notice. This had happened just prior to my project.

Geri's style of learning included many talents, but working in an office required repetitive organizational skills, high concentration and excellent sequencing skills. These were exactly the areas where Geri struggled, and at the same time presented few possibilities for her areas of strength, such as people skills, problem solving and innovation. Hopefully there is a happy ending, however, as Geri recently found a new job which involves variety, is project based and matches her need for multitasking and working in chunks, each in finite sections.

What do you think about the outcome of this case?
How could the university have responded differently?
How would your own institution react if faced with a similar case?

CASE REPORTER'S DISCUSSION

Dyslexia is not only a language difficulty but also a whole person issue. Once identified, dyslexic students such as Geri need to answer the following questions if they are to complete courses and achieve. How they *learn* to answer these questions is a shared responsibility between the teaching institution and the student.

- What is dyslexia?
- What is my type of dyslexia?
- What is my learning style?

In this case study, one of the major causes of Geri's failure was the lack of identification of her dyslexia. She was confused about her ability, her identity and her rights. Therefore if students and tutors are *dyslexia aware,* it may prevent others from having the same experience. This is a training issue where dyslexia awareness and understanding involve more than simply reading about it. Importantly, such training can create a win–win situation, releasing a more motivated learner, and possibly improving results for the institution. Dyslexia is a multi-faceted syndrome where no two students are the same, and students must understand their dyslexia profile. Often this is not addressed and the student has little or no explicit metacognition ('knowledge of how they learn').

Learning style assessment and debriefing are an aid to understanding 'self', where a student needs to recognize how differently we *all* learn. A predominantly goal oriented (future referenced), sequential learner who can manipulate abstract concepts learns in the opposite way to a predominantly present referenced, process oriented, concrete (hands-on experiential), random learner. Geri's style fits the latter description as a 'top down' learner with a holistic, 'gestalt' style of learning. Such learners need structure and time management, stimulating learning environments and study skills that use their innovative, creative intuition. Geri's natural style was also impulsive (her attention deficit) and reactive (*emotion* driven) and less reflexive and proactive (logical, sequential reasoning). Of course *we are all of these styles* but in different balances; such is the celebration of difference. But education systems, and curricula in particular, are often detailed and sequential, starting from small facts and moving up to general themes, thus creating a mismatch for many dyslexic learners who are more random and contextual learners (starting from general themes before moving down to the detail).

Bright, articulate students with dyslexia (unidentified or identified), such as Geri, risk failing in our system unless we learn to teach to all styles. Other areas to investigate are whether the learner (and teacher) is dominant in visual, auditory or kinesthetic (touch, movement and emotion). An understanding of such polar dimensions of style as concrete or abstract and sequential or random suggests that different teaching methods will be needed, even though we are all somewhere on a continuum. Geri now has information about her style, enabling her to reflect (a new experience for her) and make choices about employment and future training methods that match her style. In Geri's words, 'It [the learning style assessment] basically gave me back my confidence because I just thought I was thick, couldn't do anything. It gave me the positive attitude to get on.'

Reference

Cottrell, S (1999) *The Study Skills Handbook*, Macmillan Study Guides, Macmillan, London

CHAPTER 15

Barriers or Bridges?

Case reporter: Daniel Granger, prepared with the assistance of Dr Raymond Gonzales and Dr José Martinez-Saldana

Issues raised

This case study explores the issue of how an institution provides support for students whose background or circumstances have not prepared them for higher education.

Background

Juan and Selena are the children of Mexican-American agricultural workers in the Salinas Valley of California USA. Higher education typically had not been an option for them because of their background and circumstances. California State University Monterey Bay, founded in 1995, is committed to serving the under-served and low-income populations of California through programmes using new pedagogical approaches and infused by technology. The university has employed faculty and staff committed to this vision.

PART 1

Juan and his younger sister Selena had not been regular attendees throughout primary school. As migrant workers, their parents had had no choice but to pull them out of school every time they moved to work a new crop. Unable to read, write or speak English well themselves, their parents could not help Juan and Selena with their schoolwork. In high school, some of their schoolmates talked about going to college, and even university. Despite their inter-rupted attendance, Juan and Selena had managed to keep up in school, although just barely.

Walking home from school one day, they were chatting about their future life and education chances.

Selena said, 'Juan, I think university study must only be for people who don't have to work in the fields. Have you heard the teachers say how difficult university study is? You have to write long papers and do research. We don't have much chance anyway. Our high school advisors don't even tell us to take any of the college advanced placement courses they offer here.'

Juan wearily agreed. 'I know, Selena. When I mentioned it at home the other night, Mama yelled at me. She said I must be loco. She said college is only for those rich white people and that we live by good hard work.'

Selena then went on to tell Juan how she knew that their father would not hear of her leaving home to go away to school. 'He expects me to marry and have a family soon,' she sighed.

But Juan continued, 'You know, Selena, there's someone coming from the university tomorrow to talk to us. I haven't decided whether I'll bother to go.'

Selena urged Juan to attend the meeting.

Juan did go and so too did Selena, although she was only in her first year of high school. There were many surprises for them at the meeting. First, they heard that there were universities interested in helping students like them enrol for a degree. In fact, the university representative was from a programme called Educational Talent Search (ETS), which identified students from disadvantaged backgrounds who had the potential to succeed in higher education. Furthermore, to their surprise, the representative said he would like to work with them as they continued high school.

This was the beginning of a new way of thinking for Juan and Selena. Through Talent Search and another programme, Upward Bound, they began to realize that if they continued to study after high school, it could mean that they would get better jobs and more money to help their families. They both had previously thought that they would go to the local community college for a two-year degree; some of their friends were going, and it was so much less expensive. But the ETS counsellor explained to Juan about financial aid that was available for university. He even worked with Juan and his parents on the financial aid application.

Juan's parents were proud of him for thinking he could really go to a university. Although they were struggling financially, they insisted they would help him with his fees. But all the paperwork intimidated them, and Juan knew they could not really afford to help him financially. Juan was resigned to the fact that if he got into a university, he would have to take a job in addition to the loans he could get from Financial Aid.

Still Juan was anxious about a few things. First, he needed to get officially accepted. Then, he did not know if he would be able to do university level work. The experience of his cousin Carlos overwhelmed his thinking. Carlos had also had help from a counsellor in high school and had been admitted to one of the universities, but he had not even lasted one semester. Carlos had said that the university was like being on Mars. Everyone else seemed to know what to do and how to do it. Juan remembered how Carlos had felt lost and depressed; he had not known what he should do, or what they wanted him to do. He had not understood the assignments the instructors gave, and there were so many students in the classes that he could not ask questions. Most of his classmates had done their assignments on computers, but Carlos had only used a computer a few times in the high school lab. His freshman advisor had given him a list of courses to take without asking him about his interests. When he had told the advisor that he was worried about his language skills, he had been told when the remedial classes were offered. But Juan recalled Carlos saying that the advisor had told him that the remedial courses would not really help him toward his programme. Juan, full of uncertainty, asked himself if he was just setting himself up for a big – and expensive – disappointment.

Realistically, what are Juan's chances of succeeding?
How would your institution look on Juan as a potential student?
As a student learning support adviser, what would be your advice to Juan?

PART 2

Juan was working in the fields with his mother when the supervisor told him there was a phone call. It was his ETS counsellor. Juan's heart almost missed a beat – he had been accepted into the university!

Although he was at first excited, this news only served to intensify Juan's doubts. How could he cope with university study? However, the counsellor allayed some of his anxiety, telling him about the Summer Bridge programme offered on campus. When Juan heard that its purpose was to help students to make the transition from high school to university study, his spirits rose a little. 'At least there must be other students who need help,' he thought. Juan still wasn't sure that he could make it. But at least the Summer Bridge was a chance to see if he could even survive. If it was too tough, he could still go to the community college.

Along with the 40 other new students, Juan found that Summer Bridge was a lot of work. It was really two college courses packed into six weeks. One was an orientation to university study which included supplemental instruction in writing. The other was a computer course called Tech Tools, which taught the software and information competence skills for college study. The university 'Laptop Loaner' programme provided each student with a portable computer to use for the time they were at the university.

Juan was surprised to meet students with backgrounds similar to his own, as well as students whose earlier education had been interrupted in other ways. There were immigrants from Vietnam and Laos, as well as students from inner city schools which had not prepared them for higher education. The one thing that united all the students was that they all wanted to succeed, in spite of the unconventional paths that brought them to the university. In the orientation course, they began to understand how they might be successful. Effective communication was stressed; an explicit goal was to 'develop the ability to engage meaningfully in dialogue with people whose values, experiences, beliefs, and interests differ from their own'.

Students were encouraged to understand themselves as learners within a social context of other learners. The instructor led them in written autobiographical exercises in which they identified themselves and their backgrounds and what they had learned in that process. Some students wrote about the impact of war on their lives; others wrote about the effects of migrant work on their families, dividing them even in their citizenship, depending on which country they were in at birth. Many said that they were the first in their families to be able to read and write in English. They were all encouraged to write about that experience.

The instructor told them,

> Your background, what you've already seen and learned, shapes your perspective on everything else you learn. You need to understand your distinctive point of view. It's an important asset in tackling other challenges in unique and creative ways. Some of you are bi-lingual and even tri-lingual; you've seen this society from both the outside and the inside, and you know what it takes to make it in life. This is important knowledge that many people will never have. It adds something special to your education.

'Well,' thought Juan, 'I might have something going for me after all.' Even so, he struggled with writing; he had not been asked to do much writing in high school. But he desperately wanted to express himself. For once, he felt that someone might be listening. He worked closely with two other students to explore programmes at the university. They sometimes talked late into the night about their real experiences and interests. Juan decided to study community and human services, while his new friends LaShawn and Paulo decided on computer animation and earth science policy respectively. By the end of Summer Bridge, Juan felt much stronger. He was comfortable with his computer as a learning tool, he had made friends, and looked to his orientation instructor as a role model. When he returned home he told Selena that he would help her convince their father that she should go to university.

How would you go about designing a Summer Bridge programme?
Should a Bridge programme link to prior and further support? How?

CASE REPORTER'S DISCUSSION

The central concern of this case is the increasing number of students whose early education does not prepare them in conventional ways for higher educational study. Juan and Selena are two such examples. Their English language (second language) skills and their background did not assume advanced education in their future. Furthermore, just like many other families where there is economic hardship, wide reading and discussion was not a family activity for Juan and Selena. They had to work to contribute whatever they could to the family's finances and there was little energy in reserve for reading and discussion.

Juan was fortunate in that he came into contact with the pre-collegiate early intervention strategies, Educational Talent Search and Upward Bound. This contact and the support he received raised Juan's expectations. No longer was study beyond high school only for 'other people'; Juan began to see that it could be for him and, later on, for Selena as well. In effect, these programmes helped compensate for the absence of conventional college preparatory activities, not only in early schooling but also in students' home lives.

Raising students' expectations of their own achievement potential is a major challenge. Too often low income or minority students in secondary schools defensively pigeonhole college-bound peers as 'geeks' or 'losers'. It is then doubly difficult to convince them to want to join that group. Programmes like Educational Talent Search and Upward Bound make higher education both attractive and possible for these students. An important aspect of this process is creating peer groups to provide these students with friends and allies also interested in university study.

Juan was beset with doubts when he heard that he had been admitted to university; the negative experiences of his cousin Carlos had marked his thinking. Albeit subconsciously, Juan realized that he would need support beyond financial aid, and if he were to be successful in his studies, he needed strategies that went beyond gaining admittance. Policymakers recognize that education can help break cycles of subsistence and assist people to be integrated more effectively in society, but how can educators intervene effectively? Faculty and administrators are also obliged to maintain the academic standards of their institutions. So a university admissions director can acknowledge that these students may have the natural ability to succeed, yet still she or he must restrict university admissions to those who have mastered the knowledge and skills to undertake advanced study.

To support 'at risk' students effectively ultimately requires an institution-wide commitment. Programmes like Educational Talent Search, Upward Bound, and Summer Bridge bring students to the university. Developing confidence in their ability in a new and challenging environment is essential to firming up their commitment to this new direction. While the ETS and Upward Bound programmes assist them in deciding to 'make the leap', it is the student's first experiences on campus that make a critical difference. In particular, faculty in their courses need to continue to provide support.

Juan made friends with and found support from other students in the Summer Bridge programme. The Summer Bridge group enables new and anxious students to form friendships with peers within the context of the university. Their needs and goals are similar, and through friendship and mutual support they can work more effectively toward their individual ends. The Tech Tools course brought them together to learn to use an inherently fascinating device within the context of knowledge exploration. By the end of the summer, most of them had met the university's requirement in information skills and developed effective collaboration skills in the process.

As Juan, along with other students from the Summer Bridge programme, enrolled in his regular courses, he continued to have academic, personal, cultural and financial issues to cope with while studying. The university's extensive support network included an Academic Skills Achievement Programme providing ancillary tutoring for courses in all basic skills areas, including mathematics, critical reading, writing and technology. The Migrant Student Services programme also provided holistic support for the various interrelated issues of this group of students, also creating for them a peer support network. Juan relied heavily on this group during his first semesters at the university, then continued to participate in order to help newer students. This mirrored his growing interest in community work. For his senior capstone project in community and human services, he developed a model for accessing information about social services through computer kiosks strategically located throughout a community.

Juan found the faculty both demanding and supportive: he was expected to meet all of the course outcomes, but each instructor recognized and supported various learning approaches to those outcomes. Juan was encouraged to think and write about his experiences and how they had shaped his perspective. Such a constructivist orientation process enables students to identify and validate their own backgrounds in terms of the particular assets they bring to learning. Like Juan, they can learn to appreciate that their perspective is valid and in many ways unique. They can draw on these assets to strengthen skills needed to meet the learning goals they identify in the discovery process of the orientation course. Juan's close-knit family, for example, fostered collaboration and interpersonal negotiation skills, which made study of community and human services a natural choice for him. The other course, Tech Tools, required of all first-year students, gave Summer Bridge students a head start in learning to use a tool valuable in all their studies. This made a significant difference in their 'comfort zone' in the fall term, when they could even assist others in using a computer.

The validation of Juan's perspective raises the issue of the 'objectivity' of knowledge. It is not that there is no body of knowledge recognized as true, but that 'truth' is shared and commonly agreed and subject to change, according to experience and research. Summer Bridge enabled Juan and his classmates to join this knowledge conversation by first recognizing and articulating their own distinct voices as members of the learning community. As well as meeting students with backgrounds and experiences similar to his own, Juan came into contact with students who perceived the world from quite different perspectives. Within the supportive but challenging climate of Summer Bridge, Juan learnt that all these views were valid. He came to understand that all of these voices contribute to an ongoing inquiry into knowledge, rather than a rote acceptance of given truths. Their new skills with the computer and Internet access to extensive library resources provided a practical working tool to pursue this inquiry, just as learning to drive a car is valuable in taking a cross-country trip.

Juan had observed his cousin Carlos struggle unsuccessfully to cope with university study. When Carlos had sought assistance, his advisor had directed him to remedial courses. On many campuses, remediation is a common strategy used to address students' shortcomings in various skill areas, such as writing, mathematics, or critical thinking. Remedial courses carry either no academic credit or 'elective' credit, not contributing to students' progress toward their degrees. They are often called 'bonehead' courses or worse by students themselves. Remedial courses often can be meaningless to students, involving rote drill and practice exercises that bear no relevance to the students or their intended fields of study. Many students show no or minimal evidence of improvement on completion of such courses (McGrath and Townsend, 1997; McGrath and Spear, 1987).

In contrast, the constructivist approach to education which Juan experienced, where there was recognition that knowledge is socially constructed by each learner, suggested that each learner's background is a critical factor in effective knowledge construction. As Freire and many others have insisted, to discount or discredit that background and perspective as inappropriate for learning is, in effect, to put learners at a double disadvantage. First, they are unable to speak from their perspective, that is, to have an authentic voice in academic discussions; second, the psychological burden of the deficiency label undermines students' confidence in any of their efforts.

A constructivist approach, then, will validate the learner's identity and context, using these assets to address areas of need – building from existing strengths to bolster weaker skills. This construction is progressive, involving an overall institutional strategy. By beginning with programmes that acknowledge the distinctive background and identities of potential students, an institution encourages an alignment of personal goals with university study. In the curriculum this strategy informs individual courses as well. Faculty, especially in introductory studies, cannot assume a common student profile, and constructivist pedagogical strategies may vary according to fields, for example math versus social studies. However, a constructivist approach for all students can lead to learning experiences which are meaningful to learners, not simply the retention and rehearsal of information.

This contributed to a successful outcome for Juan. He continued with his study and is on the way to realizing his goal. But there have been additional benefits arising from his study. He and his sister have developed a Web site for his family, keeping updated information on members of the family both in Mexico and the US. They have taught their parents how to use e-mail (in Spanish). Their parents have also begun to see that Selena, too, could go to the university!

What assumptions of your institution are challenged by non-traditional students?
How does your institution deal with students with unconventional background preparation?
Are non-traditional students successful in your institutional programmes? What could you do to improve them?
Would your faculty be willing to assist in helping these students? How?

References

McGrath, D and Spear, M B (1987) The politics of remediation, in *Teaching the Developmental Education Student*, ed K M Ahrendt, pp 11–21, New Directors for Community Colleges, no 57, Jossey-Bass, San Francisco

McGrath, D and Townsend, B (1997) Strengthening preparedness of at-risk students, in *Handbook of the Undergraduate Curriculum*, ed J G Gaff, J L Ratcliff and Associates, pp 212–29, Jossey-Bass, San Francisco

TAKING THE INITIATIVE: FROM ACADEMIC SURVIVAL TO ACADEMIC SUCCESS

Case reporter: John Morley

Issues raised

This case explores the attitudes, strategies and skills that contributed to the remarkable academic success of an overseas postgraduate student who embarked on her studies with an inadequate level of English language proficiency.

Background

The case centres on the experiences of Ketmanee, a mature aged student (aged 30), who came from Thailand to Manchester University in the UK to study for an MSc leading on to a PhD in Policy Research in Engineering, Science and Technology. Ketmanee arrived in Britain in July 1997, but began her academic studies in September of the same year after having completed a 12-week pre-session course in Academic English. I am a tutor in English for Academic Purposes. I help set up and run pre-sessional courses in Academic English for international students who intend to study at Manchester, and during the academic sessions I run support classes in writing and speaking.

PART 1

I first met Ketmanee when she joined our 12-week pre-session English course in the summer of 1997. She was a hardworking and cooperative student, but she did not stand out in any remarkable way. However, her end of course report made clear that, despite the excellent progress she had made on the pre-session course, her grammar and her pronunciation were still very weak, and her vocabulary base limited. It anticipated that, as a result of these weaknesses, she would probably experience difficulties in her studies, and she was advised to seek help to improve her academic speaking and writing. These comments were not inconsistent with her earlier low TOEFL score of 473 (most universities ask for a score of 570 for undergraduate students alone), which she obtained prior to coming to the UK.

The next time I saw Ketmanee was in July last year (2000). She told me that she had completed her PhD and had been awarded Class A (in other words, there were no modifications needed), and that her department was now employing her as a researcher. I subsequently learnt that she had completed her PhD studies in the fastest time the department had known (1.8 years). In addition, her work at Manchester was described by one of her supervisors as 'a very significant undertaking', and her achievement as being 'really quite remarkable'. I was immediately impressed, not only by what she told me, but also by the degree of confidence which emanated from her. In the light of such achievements, I felt rather awkward asking her why she had not attended any of the in-sessional language support classes that we run during the academic session, and which had been recommended on her report. She told me that she had really been too busy to find time to attend, and also that attending to her academic work seemed much more important.

Intrigued, and sensing that there was a little more to her achievement than just, in the words of one supervisor, 'sheer hard work', I asked her about her experiences. How had she managed to achieve all of this?

What personal qualities might be important for someone in Ketmanee's situation?
What do you think were the actions and strategies that Ketmanee adopted?

PART 2

Through interviews with Ketmanee and her supervisors, I began to build up a picture of the factors that would eventually lead to her academic and linguistic achievements. These factors include Ketmanee's personal qualities and attitudes, and the actions and strategies that she adopted.

From speaking to Ketmanee and her supervisors, I soon became aware that she was an extremely highly motivated student. In one supervisor's words, she was very focused on her topic and it was 'almost as if she felt she had a mission. She really did work very hard – all hours'. And this sense of mission was accompanied by a very high degree of determination to succeed. He told me, 'She had a great deal of personal strength and personal courage to do the things that she did. I frankly don't know how she did it… sheer determination.'

I soon realized that Ketmanee had something of a personal point to prove. She felt that in Thailand, where she had worked as a researcher for a government funded research centre, her abilities and insights were often overlooked by senior staff and that other people, who had 'the right connections', but who she considered were less able, were promoted above her. These were the people, moreover, who tended to be sent abroad on scholarships and returned with PhDs. Ketmanee had not been selected for study abroad, but rather chose to finance herself to come here and improve professionally.

In terms of language learning, it was clear that Ketmanee had very high levels of instrumental motivation: a desire to achieve proficiency in the target language for functional or practical purposes. Interestingly, however, in the interviews, she indicated that she was fairly neutral in terms of her attitudes towards the host culture; she had no strong desire to integrate into British society, but neither was she antagonistic towards the culture, nor towards the language.

Ketmanee had already developed independent research skills, and had gained experience in managing other people. In fact, she had designed, coordinated and managed a major government/private sector research project in Thailand, and had analysed data and written reports for this. She was able to use these skills in her PhD fieldwork later. Also important, however, was the fact that she was able to apply these management skills to herself.

Her self-management skills included being able to plan and prioritize, and take the initiative in her own studies. For example, she admitted spending less time, in her first year, on her MSc assignments and instead worked on her PhD proposal (though she was not accepted onto the PhD until her MSc dissertation had been completed). As a spin-off she said she was able to relate her second semester essays to the reading she had done for her proposal and she received very high scores for these.

Ketmanee was highly self-disciplined, sticking rigidly to deadlines and often working seven days a week with only four to five hours of sleep to meet some of these. Meticulous, precise planning and goal setting were to prove indispensable in the run up to and during the data-gathering stage in Thailand. This involved making contact at a high level in the information technology (IT) industry in Thailand, organizing a series of 12 brainstorming sessions, and conducting a number of surveys within the industry. As it turned out, Ketmanee used her initiative and applied these personal management skills to her own language development.

Despite her low level of spoken English, Ketmanee made friends and networked easily with overseas students from other cultures and backgrounds. She also persuaded other people to help her. She had many friends, mainly international, both on and off her course, and the help of friends was an important factor in her achievement. For example, a friend from Mexico had allowed her to see his own PhD proposal so that she could learn more about the language and structure that was required. He also advised her to start getting her own ideas on paper in preparation for the submission of her own PhD proposal. She told me that it was only due to this advice that she was later able to have productive discussions about her proposal with her prospective supervisors.

Ketmanee took the initiative and was successful at developing networks across the university. For example, in order to become competent in certain techniques for data analysis, which according to one supervisor had never been done before, she obtained advice and input from academic staff in departments across the university. It was clear to me that Ketmanee had a great ability and desire to interact with others.

I could see that this desire was also reflected in a general openness towards other people and other people's ideas. I think this attitude was certainly helpful in her initial adjustment into the host culture, which she told me presented little of a problem for her. Ketmanee also explained that her many friends were to prove indispensable in her language development. This was not only because they provided opportunities for language practice, but also because they were happy and willing to answer her questions about the language.

Ketmanee knew that it was up to her to develop the language skills in which she knew she was weak, but which she knew she would need to develop if she were to become successful. In this way, she independently involved herself in language learning tasks. In the area of listening, for example, during her first two months in Britain she forced herself to listen to the BBC news every morning. Ketmanee also took the initiative of moving out of her accommodation, which she shared with other Thai students, after her first two months. As a result of these steps, she felt she had made a 'very big' improvement in her listening ability in a very short time.

Reading was Ketmanee's most highly developed skill, and she told me that she was already quite a proficient reader of the literature in her field before she arrived in the UK. She felt confident that she could survey references and identify the main ideas in her source texts without too much difficulty. I was impressed with this because I knew that without this initial level of proficiency in reading, it is likely that Ketmanee's task would have been very much more difficult – probably unachievable under the time constraints. Nevertheless, she was aware that she needed to broaden her knowledge of English vocabulary, and thus during her second year she scheduled a slot each morning for reading the *Financial Times*, which was available in the library.

'How would you list the four language skills in order of importance for PhD studies?' I asked her one day. This is how she listed them:

1.   Reading.
2.   Writing.
3.   Listening.
4.   Speaking.

I was not surprised at the importance Ketmanee attached to reading proficiency, given that so much of her PhD work was literature based.

Ketmanee did not spend time attending to her speaking skill during her studies. She said that her level was adequate to make friends with other overseas students, and she did not feel that she had the time to practise improving this skill. Despite this, Ketmanee was an uninhibited communicator. She was not bothered about making mistakes and poor pronunciation as long as she felt she was getting her message across. I am convinced that it was also highly significant in Ketmanee's ability to interact with and learn from others in her academic studies.

Ketmanee told me that she had been meditating every day for 15 years and she felt that this has given her two important benefits:

- Increased powers of concentration: 'that's why I am very focused and can concentrate for long periods'.
- A kind of relaxation: 'It's like sleep. Because your thought and body is totally relaxed. That's why I only need four to five hours of sleep every night.'

Ketmanee was adamant that these were essential elements in her success, and I think it would be wrong to underestimate the importance of both of these. For one thing, she really did have to work very long hours for many days to complete her work and meet deadlines. Second, she was under great stress for much of the time. The beginning of her first year was a particularly worrying time for her. Not only had her financial plans been thrown into disarray by the crash of the Thai currency at that time, but there was also a good chance that she was not going to be allowed to proceed with her PhD studies because of the poor quality of her assignments. The collapse of the currency also meant that, even if she were to be accepted onto the PhD programme, she would have to try to complete all the work in under two years, rather than three.

So all was not smooth sailing for Ketmanee, and she said that writing was where she experienced the greatest difficulties, particularly in her first year. It was principally for this reason that she scored her lowest mark for the semester on MSc coursework. She said, 'First semester, I am the lowest mark of all subjects... because I don't know how to write very well. I quite upset. I feel very depressed and very hopeless.'

In her determined way, this situation drove her to start looking at texts in a new way. She started to use her readings to look for generic patterns and structures, both linguistic and textual, in academic texts which offered possibilities for recycling in her own writing: 'reading for writing, not for information', she says. Ketmanee tells us a little about this process below, making clear that she found inspiration from readings that were not directly relevant to her own topic. She also makes clear that she was not out to copy other people's ideas:

> Something you read about human resources – it's different from my topic. I only read to see how I can adapt it for my writing.... Sometimes it's many books together... but it's not copy.

I find the following remark particularly interesting. I can see that Ketmanee has learnt to look at texts as a linguist might, by analysing a section of text in terms of its communicative function(s) and noting the language used to achieve this:

> Most of them is not relevant to my topic; it's different point but its purpose is what I want.

The technique helped her most when she wanted to begin writing:

> I find that if I can find two sentences, then I can continue with my idea. It really helpful to start writing. Often these are the first sentences.

Ketmanee told me that she found this technique tremendously useful for her and that without it she was unsure whether she could have met the deadlines that she had set for herself. Ketmanee had dozens of books and articles in her room, the pages of which had been book-marked as they contained language useful for carrying out a particular communicative function in writing. I could see that this technique was very important for her. Ketmanee's efforts did not go unnoticed. One supervisor felt there had been a significant improvement in the quality of her writing at about the time Ketmanee believed she was becoming proficient with this technique.

Are you aware of attitudes and approaches such as these in students in your support programmes?
Are there any implications of this study for your own work?

CASE REPORTER'S DISCUSSION

This study shows how a very determined person, who was not a natural linguist, whose initial English language entry score was very low, and who struggled with and remained disadvantaged by the target language throughout her PhD studies, was able to manage herself and her work, take the initiative for her own linguistic development, and utilize networking, psychological techniques and compensatory strategies which would eventually help lead to her success. One always has to be wary of drawing general conclusions from a single case study. Nevertheless, the literature suggests that most of the strategies Ketmanee adopted are not unique to her, and that they may be of considerable value to others. Student learning support programmes could well utilize Ketmanee's story. Relating her approach and experiences could act as a stimulus for international postgraduate students to actively seek solutions to difficulties they might be experiencing.

Ketmanee's utilization of language in source texts, for example, may not be unusual. In interviews with 22 overseas postgraduates (21 PhD students), Shaw found that about half claimed that they made notes of 'useful phrases in their sources texts... some kept separate sets of cards or books to enter these phrases in' (Shaw, 1991: 196). The students in Shaw's study seemed to be using source texts in a similar way to Ketmanee. Interestingly, this group, in contrast with others who felt the use of language in source texts was more of an unconscious process, had the least English in their backgrounds, and it seems that perhaps as a consequence of this, like Ketmanee, they had consciously adopted this compensation strategy.

We need to consider the pedagogical implications of this kind of exploitation of source text. For Shaw (1991: 199), 'learners can only write in an appropriate style by appropriate reading'. He goes on to suggest that the critical imitation of models and the collection of subject-specific lists of words and phrases should help learners to assimilate the conventions of 'the genre and register of their subject'. But he adds that, whilst English for Academic Purposes (EAP) tutors could help students recognize 'phrases for reuse', they also need to make students understand the difference between 'legitimate uses of models' and undesirable plagiarism. Opinions probably differ on the point at which 'creative use of source text' becomes plagiarism. How many original words, for example, can a phrase contain, and how many recycled phrases may a paragraph contain before a writer is accused of plagiarism? The University of Manchester (2001) defines 'minor' plagiarism as 'the unattributed use of a few sentences, or a short paragraph'. On this definition, Ketmanee does not appear to be guilty of plagiarism as no complete sentences were recycled. It is also worth mentioning that Ketmanee's supervisors were aware of the strategy that she was using, but had absolutely no reservations in praising the quality of the work she had done for her degree. It does raise questions for student learning support staff, though. Can they really encourage the use of a technique such as this when it would be very easy for a student to cross the line into plagiarism?

Ketmanee's use of relaxation and concentration techniques may also have much wider relevance. A quick trawl of the Internet produces a host of university health centres, self-help resource pages, counselling centres, and student support centres at universities in Britain, Australia and particularly the US, which advocate the use of meditation or relaxation exercises as a means of reducing anxiety and stress. Breathing or meditation exercises are also advocated by Oxford (1990), writing specifically about what she calls useful affective strategies for more effective language learning. Whether relaxation and concentration techniques should be added to a list of study skills covered by prospective university students on, say, a pre-session course is an interesting and debatable question. Perhaps before this, we would need to try to establish just how important these techniques are, and what kind of difference they can make to an individual's study performance; it is certainly an area that merits further investigation.

The extent to which Ketmanee corresponds to the model of the 'good' language learner by independently involving herself in language learning tasks (Naiman *et al*, 1978) also merits further consideration. For example, her improvement in listening proficiency, resulting from the independent development strategies that she adopted, is significant. She was also not afraid to make mistakes in her spoken language, and this is one of the characteristics of the good language learner, according to Ruben (1975). Other students on pre-session/EAP preparation courses need to be made aware of the value of independent learning, and should be encouraged, like Ketmanee, to develop their own individually tailored independent learning programmes.

Finally, two other relevant issues emerge from this study. One of these is the importance of academic reading proficiency for those embarking on higher degree studies, and the significance of this as an indication of a student's readiness for study. We should remember that Ketmanee claimed that she was already a reasonably proficient reader in English in her own field before she arrived in Manchester, and I believe that this was an essential factor in her achievement. Although they are not able to do anything before the student arrives to begin their studies, it seems to be good practice that pre-session/EAP preparation courses provide intensive programmes to assist in this area.

The second issue is the extent to which those who hold a PhD from an English-speaking university are expected to be proficient users of the language of study. Although Ketmanee had made an original and significant contribution to her field in a very short time, her competence as a speaker and writer of the language of studies, while undergoing considerable development, especially in writing, remained somewhat limited. However, since she has returned to Thailand and will be primarily working in the language of that country, we need to ask whether this matters. My own view is that in this case it does not; though one can perhaps think of other fields of study and situations where it clearly does.

Ketmanee's approach provides much fuel for thought for the developers of support programmes for international postgraduate students. Most importantly, it raises the question of how students can be supported and at the same time encouraged to assess their own needs and devise their own strategies to address these. Perhaps the role then becomes one of an 'independence facilitator'?

References

Naiman, N, Frohlich, M, Stern, H and Todesco, A (1978) *The Good Language Learner*, Ontario Institute for Studies in Education, Toronto

Oxford, R (1990) *Language Learning Strategies*, Hienle and Hienle, Boston, Mass.

Ruben, J (1975) What the good learner can teach us, *TESOL Quarterly*, **9**, pp 41–51

Shaw, P (1991) Science research students' composing processes, *English for Specific Purposes*, **10** (3), pp 189–206

University of Manchester (2001) Policy on plagiarism, [Online] Manchester University Web site: http://www.man.ac.uk/policies/39e.htm

SECTION 3

WORKING WITH STAFF

CHAPTER 17

LETTER OF THE LAW

Case reporter: Colin Beasley

Issues raised

The central issue in this case is how best to support the learning of first-year commerce students with the language and discourse of commercial law, especially students for whom English is a second (or additional) language.

Background

The case involves a core first-year commercial law unit during the mid-1980s at a relatively new metropolitan Australian university. It occurred just before the first intake of full-fee paying international students. Of the roughly 200 or so students enrolled, approximately 30 per cent were local and international students from culturally and linguistically diverse but predominantly Asian backgrounds. The initial course coordinator and principal lecturer was an earnest, rugby-playing 30-year-old male lawyer with no previous experience of teaching non-law students.

PART 1

John was worried. The final results were in from all the tutors who had taught in the first-year unit, Commercial Law 1 (later known as Principles of Commercial Law), which he had proudly and enthusiastically written, taught and coordinated for the first time that year. John was a new staff member who believed in maintaining high standards and was anxious to make his mark, but he was aghast at the thought that almost a third of the students had failed.

As his subject was a core or compulsory unit within the Commerce programme, this meant that all Commerce students who had failed would have to repeat it successfully next year to remain in the programme. But more worrying still was the fact that many of the students who failed were local and international students from culturally and linguistically diverse but predominantly Asian backgrounds. Furthermore, the university was currently recruiting a sizeable number of international full-fee paying students from South-east Asian countries for the first time, and it was precisely these students whom the university was hoping to attract in increasing numbers to bolster the university's financial position. It was the beginning of a new era of internationalization of higher education, and John's knowledge of Asia (he had spent some time teaching law in Hong Kong and could speak some Cantonese) was a real asset which had helped him gain his lectureship in the new and rapidly developing Commerce programme.

Damn it! He had worked hard and put together a sound course in commercial law using a reputable textbook, given comprehensive lectures and lecture notes, constructed an interesting legal problem-based tutorial programme, had well qualified tutors, and set typical assignment and exam questions that any competent first-year law student who did a bit of work should be able to pass. What had gone wrong? He hoped to get some answers from his tutors at the final tutors' meeting.

The mood at the meeting was downcast as John presented the overall grades for the unit (A, B, C, Pass and Fail). There were a number of issues concerning students on the borderline between the various grades, but these were speedily resolved through discussion between the tutors, usually on the basis of judgements about whether the students had pulled their weight in tutorials and worked hard, balanced against their performances on the written assignment and the final examination. The sticking point was the final overall 30 per cent failure rate, given that the tutors reported that nearly all their students seemed to be hard-working and capable enough, except for English language skills.

Jackie was the first to broach the subject: 'The biggest problem with some of the Asian students is English. Some of them can hardly hold a conversation with you and trying to get them to contribute to tutorial discussions is like pulling teeth.'

Roger readily agreed. 'Yeah, some of my group were the same, especially the women. But what about their writing! Some of the Asians can hardly string a grammatically correct sentence together, let alone construct an acceptable legal argument. Mind you, some of the Australian students are not much better.'

Jackie replied, 'Well, I even tried telling a number of my students that they needed to go and see someone about their English, go to some ESL (English as a second language) grammar classes for example, but I don't think many took my advice.'

Clearly something had to be done or the forthcoming international full-fee paying programme in Commerce was in jeopardy, but what, how and by whom?

What should John do?
What do you think he actually did?
What would you have done?

PART 2

John had met some of the staff in the university's learning assistance centre during orientation, and decided to phone the ESL tutor to seek help. He wanted the ESL tutor to offer assistance next year to commercial law students with language problems, but was unsure how this could best be achieved. Most students apparently had not sought out assistance when their tutors suggested it.

So when John phoned me, he was relieved that I readily agreed to help. We arranged to meet at my office in the next couple of days to talk over the matter and how best to proceed. I asked him to bring the unit materials (textbook, course outline, tutorial programme and so on) to the meeting and, if possible, samples of students' work so that I could better understand the nature of the study situation and students' difficulties.

After greeting me and taking a seat, John placed his bundle of commercial law materials on the table and, with a hint of agitation, opened one of the sheath of exam scripts he had brought along. 'Take a look at this,' he said dramatically, pointing to the confused scrawlings in not very fluent or grammatical English and the meagre mark that it had attracted in the margin of the student's exam booklet. He explained that, 'I have dozens more just the same. One in three students failed the course, so I really hope you can help. My tutors tried to encourage their weaker students to come here for help but it appears that strategy has not been very effective at all.'

'Well, I don't have any magic wand or miracle cure, but I am sure that we can work something out,' I replied with a smile. I explained to John that I was not surprised that some students were reluctant to seek help, as there can often be a loss of face involved. No one likes to be singled out and told they have a problem that they need to go off to a stranger to 'get fixed', I suppose. I explained the philosophy of our centre, where we prefer, if we can, to work with students' language and learning problems and needs in the context of their programme of study, rather than in isolation, because we believe that teaching skills in context is much more effective. Then I came to the sensitive point. Would John be prepared to provide ongoing assistance and advice? After all, his job description did not state that he had to spend extra time working with staff in the learning assistance centre. I told him that if I could have his ongoing assistance and involvement, I was confident that with a bit of work we could come up with an effective support programme.

John's relief at a positive strategy was obvious. The issue of extra work did not even seem to have entered his mind. 'Great,' he said. 'I'd be more than happy to give you whatever assistance you need.'

I explained that I would need a full set of unit materials to analyse and study in order to develop relevant support material. I would have to dive into the deep end with the language and discourse of commercial law, which would be a challenge as I had no academic background or previous experience in law or legal studies. So I told him I was sure that I would have to run my ideas past him from time to time to check that they were accurate and appropriate. I also mentioned that I wanted to attend all the unit lectures the next year to get a first hand idea of the likely problems, particularly for ESL students, with learning the law. I wanted to organize a convenient time when most students would be available (so it would not clash with any of their tutorials) and run weekly support workshops which would largely follow the content sequence and assessment demands of the unit. I told him that I knew he was very busy, but if he could attend these sessions as well, then conceptual issues could be dealt with as well as language ones. I told him to have a think about it and let me know his thoughts.

What do you think will be the main problems faced by John and Colin (the ESL tutor?)
How do you think the students will react to the extra classes?

PART 3

We met again after the university vacation. I asked John if he remembered our previous conversation about running a series of support workshops for commercial law students, and asked if he would be able to be involved. After a moment's reflection, he replied, 'Count me in.'

Thus began a fruitful ongoing working relationship between myself and not only John, but also subsequent coordinators of Principles of Commercial Law. John provided me with copies of textbooks and all unit materials, as well as other very useful books and support material related to themes and tasks in the course. I attended all the unit lectures and analysed the unit textbook and handout materials, immersing myself in the discourse of commercial law with the express aim of identifying likely problems, particularly for ESL students. Although his schedule was pretty crowded, John readily agreed to attend the support sessions, and together we worked out a couple of possible times which we hoped would also suit interested students. Because of the amount of preparation and liaison involved, especially initially, it was decided that the support classes would not begin until after the introductory topics and the first non-teaching break of the semester (ie until teaching week 5). After deciding on a suitable time and venue, the sessions were advertised at the beginning of the commercial law lectures in the early weeks of the semester, with John enthusiastically introducing me and encouraging ESL students to attend.

Interested students were asked to sign up on the learning assistance centre's noticeboard. A total of 34 students attended some of these classes between week 5 and the final week of semester, week 13. Although the commercial law support classes were voluntary, the attendance figures held up quite well over the nine weeks (the average attendance per session being 12), certainly better than at some general support classes like grammar, essay writing and the like, attendances at which often fell to unsustainable levels towards the end of the semester as students' focus shifted squarely to the final exams.

John proved a wonderful colleague to work with and I felt that we made a good team. He enthusiastically attended every support session, which benefited from the different perspectives we both brought to the materials and topics of the course. The support programme focused on the course outline and assessment tasks of the unit. John provided very useful extra materials on reading and analysing statutes, answering legal problem questions, and the basic concepts and principles of contract law. So in consultation with John, I prepared exercises and activities to explore both the language and logic of legal discourse and improve students' skills at analysing and writing in law, and succeeding in the assessment tasks of the unit. Particular attention was paid to analysing and answering legal problem questions, because not only was this a new genre, quite different from essays, which all students had to master, but also this genre predominated in the assessment tasks of the unit: in tutorials, written assignments and the final examination.

Because of the centrality of the legal problem, I asked John if he could write a suggested answer to one of the tutorial questions to use for teaching purposes, which he readily did. This, and other suggested answers to past assignment, tutorial and exam questions provided by John and subsequent lecturers, proved extremely useful for students as novice writers to develop skills and understanding in analysing and composing appropriate answers to legal problem questions. These expert texts provided me as the language and learning specialist with invaluable material to analyse the salient features of the discourse needing to be explained to the students, in terms of both linguistic features and cognitive strategies. It was also invaluable to be provided copies of excerpts of good and not so good answers by students to assignment and exam questions when conducting review sessions. Although these tasks all demanded extra time and input from the subject specialist, this all led to great benefits for the students and subsequently to the overall design and teaching of the whole unit, as many materials, ideas and activities developed for the support tutorials became incorporated over time into the mainstream course.

An immediate issue for some staff (and students) was the perception that the ESL students were getting an unfair advantage in terms of teaching input and resources. It was resolved, therefore, that future classes would be open to any student who wanted to attend, with tutors particularly encouraging students experiencing language and learning difficulties to attend. The end of semester results reassuringly were nowhere near as drastic as those of the previous year, and students who had attended the support classes with any regularity all passed.

The following year, the support classes commenced in the second week of semester and ran in tandem with the mainstream tutorials for the entire semester. They were open to anyone interested, and two sessions per week had to be scheduled due to demand. Indeed, the attendance and enthusiasm increased so much (30-plus students on occasions) that more sessions would have been desirable, but these were not scheduled because of concern about the extra time commitment required of the course coordinator. The support programme continued to be refined with the cooperation and involvement of three subsequent course coordinators over several years. Students consistently evaluated the support classes as very useful, and the unit failure rates became much more modest.

The present coordinator has redesigned the unit quite substantially, incorporating explicit instruction and guidance in answering legal problems in the mainstream tutorials and an initial practice assignment in this genre. Consequently, students are performing better and the semester-long support programme has been discontinued in favour of two strategically timed workshops. One is held just before the first test and the other before the main assignment.

What do you think of the outcome?
Do you think that anything should have been done differently?
Are there any implications for your own work?

CASE REPORTER'S DISCUSSION

This case concerns strategies for dealing effectively with the language and learning difficulties of students studying commercial law, especially for students from culturally and linguistically diverse backgrounds. It provides support for the notion that language and learning skills are more productively addressed in the context of students' actual programmes of study rather than in isolation. It also demonstrates that successful collaboration between subject specialists and language and learning professionals is advantageous not only for students experiencing difficulties, but also for the teaching staff. Indeed, it can lead, as it did in this case, to better curriculum design and teaching practices from which all students can benefit.

Students from non-English speaking backgrounds who are directed by their lecturers and tutors to go to see an ESL tutor to 'fix up' their grammar and writing skills are unlikely to gain the necessary linguistic and cognitive skills required to perform complex academic tasks in their disciplinary study, such as writing successful answers to legal problem questions. Indeed, they may never even make it to the tutor. This strategy was singularly unsuccessful initially in this case study. The preferred approach of the learning assistance centre at the author's university is to integrate language and study skills instruction with course content, as this increases student motivation in developing appropriate skills and also reduces problems of transferring skills to required learning tasks (see Beasley, 1990).

The lecturer in this case study was prepared to work together collaboratively with a language and learning professional and invest extra time and energy on an ongoing basis to develop a learning programme better tailored to students' actual language and learning needs. The study of law often involves making fine distinctions based on the interpretation of language and competing points of view, and thus poses linguistic and learning challenges for all students, but particularly for students from non-English language and cultural backgrounds. Students have not only to learn 'a new language', the language of the law with its peculiar terminology and discourse, but they also have to adjust to a different way of thinking and develop new learning styles to understand the principles and complexity of legal interpretation and argument. As one law lecturer puts it, 'Understanding the way in which language is used to explain the logic behind legal arguments requires the re-orientation of thought patterns' (Yamouni, in Crosling and Murphy, 1994: v).

However, these skills and strategies are rarely explicitly taught to students because of what has been called the 'paradox of expertise', the fact that most experts in a discipline are generally not consciously aware of the skills and strategies that they employ. As Lundeberg (1987: 409) puts it, 'experts who engage in a process automatically probably do not know how they know what they know'. An important task of the language and study skills professional at tertiary level, therefore, is to provide activities and materials that help make the experts' strategies and the discourse conventions of the genres within a disciplinary culture explicit and accessible to students. As this case study shows, the ongoing collaboration between John (and subsequent course coordinators) and myself enabled a learning programme to be developed which could identify appropriate strategies and generic conventions relevant to legal discourse, such as writing answers to legal problems, and explicitly teach these to students.

This kind of collaboration requires a considerable and ongoing commitment on both sides, in terms of time and energy. John was prepared to make that commitment, and a very productive relationship developed which led not only to successful outcomes for the students who attended the extra support classes, but also ultimately to better teaching outcomes overall, as more and more ideas and activities developed and utilized in the support classes were taken up in the mainstream unit. The case study also demonstrates that although a support programme may originally be conceived in terms of better meeting the needs of particular students, in this case students from culturally and linguistically diverse backgrounds, it can be beneficial for any student in the course.

References

Beasley, C J (1990) Content-based language instruction: helping ESL/EFL students with language and study skills at tertiary level, *TESOL in Context*, **1**, pp 10–14

Crosling, G M and Murphy, H M (1994) *How to Study Business Law: Reading, writing and exams*, Butterworths, Sydney

Lundeberg, M A (1987) Metacognitive aspects of reading comprehension: studying understanding in legal case analysis, *Reading Research Quarterly*, 22, pp 407–32

CHAPTER 18

ACADEMIC FRIEND OR FOE?

Case reporter: Monique Osborn

Issues raised

The issue addressed in this case is how a learning assistance support person can enter a difficult academic environment and develop relationships with teachers to effect change.

Background

The case took place in the School of Engineering of a rural campus of Monash University in Australia. The institution had evolved from a college of advanced education, to a university college and finally to a campus of an established university. The campus's rural setting enabled small class sizes and a more personal approach to university life. The case reporter was involved in supporting a group of engineering academics concerned about the effectiveness of their teaching and student learning.

PART 1

At first, my attempts to blend into the university engineering community were not always positive experiences. As a student learning support academic, my role was to assist students and teaching staff with issues concerning effective learning and teaching. But as a non-engineering academic, I had often met with negative body language while strolling through the engineering school as I attempted to initiate informal conversations regarding teaching and learning.

'I'm numeracy based, not literacy,' one engineering academic said as he declined my offer to work collaboratively with him in his first-year class. Another insisted that he needed little preparation: 'The order of my lecture jumps around according to how the overheads fall out of the folder,' he explained. 'Are you serious?' I asked, thinking that this was his attempt at humour. 'Yes! That's the plan, because then you can talk about anything. My mind is not really structured and I really don't care where I go.' He then tried to reassure me with, 'But in the end I keep pulling it all back together.' I hid my shocked response. Did this academic ever question the effectiveness of his teaching in relation to his students' learning?

I was beginning to understand why the Dean of Engineering had allocated funds to the learning support unit on the campus to look into teaching practices in an attempt to address the increasing attrition rate of first-year undergraduates. I was also not surprised that this was given priority. Through my position, I was aware of the considerable misalignment of some teaching practices and student learning. Both Australian and international students often complained to me about the ineffectiveness of the teaching. On the other hand, academics often stated their dissatisfaction with the standard of student work. My somewhat lengthy affiliation with this institution, first as a student and then as an academic, also helped me to realize that many of the academic staff did not have formal teaching qualifications. I thought this absurd: how could anyone teach effectively without a pedagogical framework?

As is often the case in a tertiary education setting, the decision to change was not collaborative. Policies to ensure accountability and accreditation generally are formulated and implemented in a top-down approach and, particularly as this was a rural campus, in an outside-in manner. As a result, staff often felt resentful of having to change their individual teaching behaviour that they had established over many years. When this was combined with my non-technical background, I knew that my job of integrating student learning services into the School of Engineering would be challenging. In fact, I often felt more like an 'academic foe' than an 'academic friend'.

Fortunately an opening appeared. The Head of School invited me to join the staff in a two-day staff development seminar based on 4MAT® (McCarthy, 1987). Leon, a senior academic staff member who also acted as head at times, actually approached me for assistance to implement problem based learning. It seemed that my persistence had paid off.

Leon had transferred from industry to teaching in the engineering faculty more than 15 years earlier and had not had any formal professional development on pedagogical issues. So he and I had plenty to talk about, and our discussions arising from our first meeting gave me some insight into engineering academic life. Leon explained to me that informal discussions within the school were not usual for two main reasons. The first was that teaching and learning practices were not considered important, and the second was that discussions with colleagues about problematic issues were often interpreted as a sign of weakness. Leon explained as follows:

> A good number of years ago in fluids I had people using a technique till I thought it was coming out of their ears and they would be terrific when I got them again in third year. But when I did [hand movement over head] whoosh, it's not there.... What that helped me to see... not that it was a solution... it gave me a message that something was not working, because you had taught your heart out in this area [but] I probably cried in my beer and did the same thing next year because I didn't know any different.

The more I talked to Leon, the more I realized that he was a rare breed of engineering academic: he was self- reflective and appreciated the complexities of learning and teaching. He commented that:

> It's too hard to pitch to a person... who may have a different learning style from myself. In terms of effectiveness, I can recognize that it is rather like throwing a handful of grain at the barn door and hoping that some will hit it. So you think to yourself, this is not a well thought out process.

I decided that it was important to nurture these qualities in Leon and that suggesting he attend off campus ad hoc professional development courses would not benefit him. He had already told me of his previous experiences in this type of professional development:

> I walked away with 20 good ideas and no time or help to implement them... I need some tools... I don't need more information. I need to take the information and have someone to help me structure it in a way that is going to help me in tomorrow's lecture.

I knew that our relationship was a start. But I also knew that the bigger problem was how I could assist Leon to develop effective teaching practices in a school that did not promote collegial assistance. How could the development of teaching practices be given priority in a school where no academic had formal pedagogical training?

What do you think the student support academic should do?
How do you think she could help Leon?
What can be done with regard to the school as a whole?

PART 2

I decided that the best way to address the situation was to use the knowledge and experience I had acquired from my previous position as a supervisor of student teachers on practicum. Perhaps it was possible to work collaboratively with Leon in his tutorials to see at first hand how he went about his teaching? However, a technical and non-technical teacher sharing a common teaching space did not happen regularly in this school. I seriously considered that I could be setting myself up for a disaster, knowing that the students would be questioning my role in their engineering tutorials. I had already begun to understand that anything out of the ordinary seemed to cause anxiety for both the teaching staff and the students.

Further, it was clear that there were differences in Leon's and my ways of thinking, and this could also lead to conflict. Leon was the logical sequential processor and wanted to slowly piece ideas together, while I generally prefer a holistic view and dismantle the pieces as the need arises. Perhaps that is why one of our initial conversations concerning the student learning outcomes of his teaching session led to Leon's comment: 'For all I know you are describing the beaches in Greece,' insisting that my questions and comments were incomprehensible. At that point I was beginning to wonder whether I was the right person to assist Leon.

Again, fortunately for me, Leon had a supportive working relationship with colleagues who were also teaching the common first-year civil engineering unit. Sue and Philip had also shown some interest in improving teaching and learning practices. Although I knew that Leon was feeling frustrated with the whole venture, he still had a spark of interest and invited Sue and Philip to work with us.

Sue and Philip agreed to join, and so our network was born. The two-day staff development seminar that we had all attended helped us to recognize our preferred learning practices. Leon was the 'analyst', always seeking to understand working components. 'If you have to understand a particular area of theory and then function with it… you need an understanding of the framework and you need functionality and depth of each component within it.' Sue was similar to Leon, but felt stifled by subjects independently planned off campus. She said that, 'Teaching this subject was the worst experience that I had ever had. I didn't have control over it…. It was timed to a very rigid guideline. It wasn't flexible as other subjects, where I could change the content as I went.'

As a discerning practitioner, Sue was also looking for answers:

What can I do to take more control over this subject as well as maintaining similar outcomes to the other campuses? What happens if I spend more time on questioning and less time on providing content? What can I do about students who leave tutorials early?

Sue's focus obviously complemented Leon's. As Philip was not directly involved with the teaching of the common first-year civil engineering unit he became 'the overseer' for the network. His teaching and mentoring approach was typically integrative and collaborative.

I had multiple roles. As an active participant, I was the coordinator. As a passive researcher I could determine the effectiveness of the approach. Metaphorically, I equated myself to an 'electrical adapter', enabling people individually or collectively to access a common source. As contact with Leon, Sue and Philip was both continual and intermittent, I needed to take a flexible approach, adopting different roles as the situation required.

Fortunately, my participation in tutorials was readily accepted by academics and students, although it did not take too long for the students to fathom my incompetence in civil engineering. It soon became apparent to them that I could not provide much assistance in their bridge construction activities! But once Leon and Sue explained why I was there, the students soon came to trust me. This was an added bonus. I could now discuss the effectiveness of teaching practices with students and with their lecturers within the working environment.

After recounting my observations and our informal discussions, Leon and Sue began to experiment with their teaching practices. This was very exciting for them and they soon began to feel empowered about their teaching and their students' learning. They had not experienced this as a result of the off campus professional development workshops they had previously attended. In fact, Leon described these as a time-wasting exercise, as individual needs were not addressed and printed materials were rarely referred to or used.

As time progressed, we all began to see that we needed to extend our network beyond the university staff. For example, our discussions about transition issues were somewhat stymied, and we needed information about students' previous educational experiences, which called for the involvement of secondary teachers. Our rural community was close and relatively small, and our campus was surrounded by several feeder secondary schools. It therefore seemed logical to try to find out how teaching practices in the two sectors differed.

This was a common sense approach, but it was also a challenge. Generally, staff from the university worked in secondary schools in advisory roles, but rarely did secondary teachers provide professional development for academics. Reg and Richelle, teachers at one of the schools, reluctantly volunteered to join our discussion group. 'What could I possibly do to help a university lecturer?' exclaimed Richelle. Reg was also concerned: 'Are we overstepping the mark here, doesn't the university provide professional development?' Despite their initial concerns and lack of confidence in their ability to assist with university teaching, it turned out to be a very rewarding venture. They provided us with useful information about learning in their sector, and we provided them with the same from our setting. The bridge was being built from both sides. and over time our discussions covered problem based learning, classroom management, and questioning and learning expectations. Our implementation of changes undoubtedly benefited from our sharing of experiences and joint learning in our initial engineering network, as well as from the inclusion of our colleagues from the secondary setting. We also know that management in the Engineering Department was quietly pleased with our achievements overall.

CASE REPORTER'S DISCUSSION

Arguably, university academics have been valued for their research skills and content knowledge, and professional development has mainly been concerned with this. Furthermore, the degree of student learning has generally not been the responsibility of the tertiary educator if the content has been consistently 'delivered'. This was the situation I faced in the Engineering Department. The long-standing mind set had not encouraged engineering academics to consider or value pedagogical issues and their teaching. It was even more disheartening that for those who were beginning to have questions, supportive assistance was not readily at hand. It was clear to me that the engineering staff's lack of awareness of teaching issues was increasing within the faculty and had not been confronted.

My position as an outsider to the faculty, although a longstanding member of the rural community, had advantages. First, I could draw on my extensive professional network, within and outside the university. This made it easier to recruit secondary school staff such as Reg and Richelle. Second, I could contribute objectively to an in-house faculty problem. I also did not have to travel long distances from another campus to do this. I also had the imprimatur of the head of school, which added value to my position!

Furthermore, I was not a stakeholder in the faculty and thus my views did not threaten anyone's position. Of course, I had to operate with sensitivity, but I think that my teaching experience meant that being diplomatic was almost second nature to me in professional settings.

Another option would have been for someone with an engineering background to undertake the staff development, but it seems that people with backgrounds in both teaching and learning issues and engineering are not easy to come by. Many engineering staff on the campus had come directly from industry and did not have an educational background. Other civil engineering staff were located on other campuses over 150 kilometres away and this greatly limited the possibility for regular face to face communication. Admittedly, as a non-technical person, there was a communication barrier, but my research activities, teaching skills and persistence assisted me, and in the long run this was not a major issue.

A further option to the work-embedded programme would have been formal professional development short courses. In endeavours to enhance the quality of learning and teaching, a large range of professional development courses was available. Teaching staff were encouraged to seek assistance from the centres involved in higher education research and development. A major drawback to these courses, however, was that they were most often held on other campuses and involved a transmissive approach. This had not proved to be suitable for Leon and his colleagues, as they said that such programmes were limited in how they could address their needs. Thus, they continued to use what could be seen as inadequate teaching strategies. Another drawback, as expressed by Leon, was that the presenters of such programmes generally assumed the learning needs of the participants, and little or no follow-up assistance was provided.

For some, staff or professional development of this nature is effective in encouraging them to reflect on the effectiveness of their teaching. But for others, as in Leon's case, the course materials were more often left to collect dust and had little impact on teaching practices. As Leon also hinted, such short courses were an uncomfortable experience and further entrenched in their minds their futility. For me, this was another reason to consider the benefits of work-embedded professional development, as I saw it as a way of effectively meeting individual professional needs as they arose.

The work-embedded approach was also in accord with the culture of the rural campus. Formal and informal supportive networks for students and staff are an integral part of the way things work. The region's rural culture also meant that the relationships could be extended beyond the university if necessary, as occurred with the secondary staff in relation to transition to university study issues. The work-embedded approach draws on trust between participants and it unravels slowly as issues arise. In this way, it allows self-empowerment to develop over time. But it does require time to acknowledge the power and parity of each participant, and this could be seen as a disadvantage. I also had to be flexible in my role, as sometimes I was a mentor, sometimes an assistant, sometimes a 'scaffolder' or even a 'parent'. In relation to Reg and Richelle, I was at times like a 'parent' as I boosted their confidence that they had something important to offer to the university teachers. Afternoon teas that I provided proved to be a good source of comfort for the social aspect of this, and off-campus short courses cannot compete with them. Leon, Sue and Philip appreciated the work-embedded assistance; it was a nurturing and supportive environment for them to develop their teaching approaches.

In the work-embedded approach, we had to confront each other's different learning approaches. Initially, when Leon and I faced our differing styles, it would have been easy for us to acknowledge these and move away to find others with whom we were more compatible. Fortunately, we were able to move through this and appreciate the value of different approaches, and in fact we all gained from it and could widen our approach by incorporating aspects of the other style. When it came to working with Sue and Philip, we were comfortable enough to be able tacitly to allocate each other roles so that we all felt valued.

Initially it was not surprising that the engineering students openly questioned my presence in their tutorials. A collaborative and frank explanation enabled me to elicit ongoing valuable information regarding the appropriateness of teaching practices without threatening the credibility of academics and students. The fact that we were modelling the flexibility required of teachers who need to accommodate a variety of learning approaches in their students made the project an 'authentic' learning experience for us as staff.

However, there were also disadvantages. What we did was time-consuming and is therefore costly. It required ongoing support both within and out of the teaching environment, so that the teaching strengths could be identified and nurtured and weaknesses improved on. Observation and discussion also need to be ongoing, so that trust and confidence are maintained. But in this case the benefits far outweighed the disadvantages, as the teachers were empowered to value their teaching. An incidental benefit was that it also encouraged other engineering staff to speak out more confidently about their teaching and learning needs, particularly those undertaking a Graduate Certificate of Tertiary Teaching offered off campus. Furthermore, informal discussions with academics from other faculties about this experience also generated a keen interest in similar support.

In our work-embedded network, we were all intrinsically motivated to further develop effective teaching practices. This was evidenced by our persistence, despite initial difficulties. Without this intrinsic motivation any professional development approach would be futile. Traditionally, professional development has been seen as a catalyst for change in teaching behaviour, but our experiences are that professional development can only act as a support towards self-empowerment.

The success of a work-embedded approach depends on the commitment and input of the participants. A major advantage is that new approaches can be experimented with in a supportive environment. It also means that student input is valued, and this is something perhaps not taken advantage of by traditional staff development. Initially these engineering academics were seeking the formula which would 'revolutionize' teaching and learning. It soon became apparent that assisting academics to maximize student learning was a lengthy, intricate but rewarding process. It became most apparent that not all students 'pick things up along the way or osmotically'. It is clearly an immense responsibility of the tertiary academic to assist students to achieve set learning outcomes. In this case mutual dedication from teaching staff and students led to improved attainment of learning outcomes. After all, there can be no teaching without students, and they are a necessary side of the teaching and learning coin.

Reference

McCarthy, B (1987) *The 4 Mat System: Teaching to learning styles with right and left mode techniques*, EXCEL, USA

CHAPTER 19

GENERALIZING THE GENERIC

Case reporters: Glenda Crosling and Alan Farley

Issues raised

The issues in this case concern the role of a learning skills adviser in a major faculty initiative explicitly to teach and assess generic or lifelong learning skills.

Background

This case occurred in a faculty of a large Australian university. The faculty concerned had six discipline-based departments and about 10,000 students based on five Australian campuses. Bill had been the Associate Dean, Undergraduate Teaching, for three years. Cheryl has been the Faculty Transition and Generic Skills Adviser on a part-time basis for three years and was also the faculty learning skills adviser on the largest campus. She had worked in the field of student learning support for more than a decade.

PART 1

Bill looked pensive. His faculty had to refocus its approach and make explicit the teaching and assessment of generic or lifelong learning skills. Anyone in Bill's situation would be pensive! He was responsible for the programme which he knew would create anxiety among teaching staff. They already taught large numbers of students as well as researching and publishing, and this would be seen as yet another task to add to the list.

Bill's concerns were real. The faculty operated on five campuses, with more than 10,000 students. There were three degree 'families', six discipline-based departments, and eleven generic skills to be considered. As the Faculty Transition and Generic Skills Adviser and student learning support academic, it was my job to assist Bill. We both recognized that there was plenty of work ahead of us.

Implementation of generic skills was part of the university's Learning and Teaching Plan. Faculties were 'lead sites' for various aspects of the plan and acted as examples for other faculties, who would implement similar programmes later. The Faculty of Business was the lead site for generic skills. Students would need to demonstrate a minimum standard in these skills before graduation, including written communication, oral communication, critical analysis, team work and information literacy. Although the task was daunting, I knew that Bill was very good at taking a systematic and 'helicopter' view of this large faculty's curriculum, and that would stand us in good stead.

We also knew that we were not alone and that all universities were focusing on students' generic skills and graduate attributes. These had become significant in the higher education 'quality' agenda, and employers and the community had expectations of universities in this area. Employers wanted graduates with good generic skills, as well as technical expertise in their fields. So, although daunting, it was an important job for us to take on. This is what I was thinking about as Bill and I had our first conversation about the project.

I said, 'This will be good for our students. The international students can become lost when they're confronted with a critical, analytical approach and the mature aged students need assistance, especially if they're working and studying at the same time. A clear focus on skills will really help a lot of our students.

But how are you going to manage it over such a large faculty? How can the six disciplines and the range of skills be accommodated? We know that the disciplines emphasize the skills differently. Critical thinking is seen differently in management and econometrics.'

Bill replied, 'We can't just impose this on staff. It has to be an inclusive process.'

At the first meeting of the faculty Learning and Teaching Plan Committee the members' comments indicated the rough terrain ahead. 'Don't we already teach and assess these skills, and haven't we always done this?' asked John, who had taught at the university for more than 30 years. 'What are they on about this time?' There seemed to be general agreement with this comment.

'And what about the work load that will come from all this?' said Mary. 'Who's going to tell the staff they have to do this?'

How would you react to these questions?
What approach would you take towards this task?

PART 2

Bill's reply was perfect. 'That's why we have to do an audit of the curriculum. Let's find out where we are in relation to these skills. Then we'll know if it will be a big job, or a smaller job. But we have to find out.'

I tried to contextualize the project from a learning skills perspective. 'Our student profile has changed. It's not that our students can't do these things, but they need assistance to "read" the culture, to understand the important aspects. If they are clearer on what we want, I think our teaching jobs will be more fulfilling.'

It was decided that the first step was to survey the 125 leaders of large subjects across the undergraduate degree. We would inquire if various skills were relevant to their subject, if and how they were assessed, if the skill was taught, and how. We also tried to pin down interpretations across the departments of what they meant when they talked about the skills. 'If we are going to teach and assess them,' I said, 'we need to know what we mean by them.'

Response to the survey was adequate at more than 40 per cent. 'We can at least say that the data are representative and make some valid conclusions,' commented Bill.

Bill was pleased with the survey results. 'We're doing well overall,' he told the committee at the next meeting. 'Generally, the skills are already being taught and assessed across the faculty curriculum.' So rather than imposing new demands for teaching and assessment in the curriculum, the plan was to make what was already there more explicit. Of course, refinements, additions and standardization would be needed, but these could build on the existing basis. 'This is great,' I thought. I knew that our students were capable, but I also knew that many would cope much better if we emphasized our expectations systematically. It would also mean that there would be a clearer and integrated foundation for my learning skills and transition work.

One committee member commented under her breath in the meeting, 'How do we know that the survey responses really are what they do in their teaching and assessment?' It was a good point, but the data seemed convincing enough to continue with the implementation. Bill then presented the next steps to the committee for discussion.

The process would have two stages, building on the faculty's six compulsory subjects in all programmes, one from each department. First, through the compulsory subjects, the skills would be introduced, taught, assessed, and students given feedback at a basic level. Students who were below the level would be directed to support services and materials to develop their skills. The second stage would rely on the pattern of skills development and testing across other subjects throughout the programmes. This would mean a high likelihood that students could not successfully complete the programme without demonstrating an acceptable level in all the skills. As the survey had revealed that much of stage two was already in place, stage one was where the substantial work was needed. The initial introduction and development of skills would be integrated into the early classes in the compulsory subjects. Testing and feedback would become part of the existing assessment for these subjects.

It seemed like a straight forward plan, but the meeting discussion was confused. Several issues needed resolution. How could the skills be covered across the six subjects/departments and the five Australian campuses? Clearly, all departments could not cover all the skills in their introductory subjects. How could skills be allocated to particular subjects or departments? The survey data were useful, but far from complete. Although they showed which of the disciplines focused on particular skills, there were inconsistencies across campuses and disciplines. Accounting and Finance focused on teamwork through group assignments on one campus, but not on others. Fortunately, there were some consistencies. Management and Business Law scored highly on written communication, Marketing on oral communication, Economics and Management on academic enquiry, critical thought and team work, while Econometrics, not surprisingly, focused on numeracy. Information literacy was attributed to Management and Accounting. Here at last was something to work with!

The uncertainty in the meeting soon indicated clumsiness in dealing with 11 skills separately across six departments. The skills had to be simplified and grouped into six units. Each department could then focus on one set of skills. Discussion on the groupings was long and frustrating, but finally, six groups were agreed: written communication; oral communication; critical thought, analysis and problem solving; academic enquiry, research and information literacy; numeracy; and use of technology. Now we could think of the skills in relation to particular departments.

The teaching staff obviously knew their disciplines, whereas I had an overall view of the departments from my student learning work. I could stand back, read the culture, assess the values and make suggestions. And that is exactly what I did. Even so, Bill realized that a standardized approach across the campuses was not possible, as all campuses had their strengths and preferences. Skills would need to be allocated to departments according to their strengths in the introductory subjects on particular campuses.

The way was now clear for defining the skills. We had rich data from the survey because subject leaders had indicated their interpretation of what each skill meant in their area. So we could profile the skills across departments and chart the subtle differences. For instance, for written communication, Management emphasized supporting points with evidence, establishing a clear purpose in the written piece, and addressing the task. For Business Law, the emphasis was on using clear English expression, developing or explaining a response clearly, and concluding clearly.

The groundwork was then completed for stage one: skills were grouped and defined and departments on particular campuses allocated sets of skills for the introductory subjects. But there was still much to do. Academic staff needed to be encouraged to participate, and skills needed to be written into the assessment tasks. Academic staff required training to assess the skills, the skills needed to be taught and students' attention directed to their importance. Materials needed to be assembled and developed so that students could access instruction utilizing flexible modes. More work was needed on integrating development and testing of the skills into later year subjects, and explicit statements about the skills would also be required so that students appreciated their importance. Learning skills work would be linked more directly with the faculty's generic skills programme.

Do you think this is an appropriate way of implementing the generic skills in the curriculum?
How would you encourage staff to implement such a scheme? What training do you think academic staff would need?

CASE REPORTERS' DISCUSSION

The case indicates the change involved in integrating generic skills in the curriculum. John remarked in the first committee meeting that these skills are hallmarks of a university education anyway, so why should they need to be explicitly taught and assessed? We knew, however, that times and the student profile had changed, and issues of quality and competitiveness were at the forefront. The central issue of the case is therefore how a systematic approach could be developed to support student learning by explicit teaching and assessment of generic skills.

Bill's macro level view guided his approach. The approach had to be suitable for a large, multi-campus faculty, in order to ensure some degree of consistency. An alternative approach might have been to suggest that interested staff include teaching and assessment of some of the skills in the subjects they taught. These might then have stimulated other staff to try similar things. But this was working from the micro level and would have taken time to develop across departments and campuses. Also, the brief was to implement the skills across the curriculum at all levels. The systematic, macro-level approach therefore seemed to be the most sensible.

In order not to impose too much on the time of teaching staff, we used consultation through the committee and given the culture of the faculty and the way it operated through management levels, this appeared to be a suitable couse of action. The committee members also taught across the departments, and it is likely that they would talk about what was being done at the committee level in their departments. This would flag and prepare staff to some extent for the changes.

Another more inclusive approach would have been to call for interested staff, to join the committee. A disadvantage, though, would have been that such staff would not necessarily have had the authority to implement the changes, and might not have been familiar enough with the working of their departments to make informed decisions. Perhaps the use of focus groups could have led to a more inclusive approach by feeding into the main committee through representatives. But again, this could have been a drawn-out and complicated process.

The importance of staff taking a positive approach to the scheme was clear to both Bill and me. If they were not committed, it would devolve to nothing more than tokenism. Bill's approach, supported by the survey data, was positive. Rather than emphasizing deficit, he focused on what had been done and was already in the curriculum in relation to generic skills. Therefore, the next step was adjusting and standardizing, rather than introducing. Change would still be required, however, as generic skills would need to be written into the assessment tasks. Staff would need to evaluate their students' performance on these tasks, and while some staff would already be familiar with assessing some of the skills, others would not.

Turning to the procedure, a question arises about the validity of using a survey to audit the curriculum. As one committee member commented, how could we be sure that what was claimed in the survey was the reality? Furthermore, the survey mainly delivered quantitative results. Although the survey included a final section for respondents' comments, it did not deliver the same richness of data that could be obtained through interviews or focus groups.

Again, an alternative might have been to form staff focus groups. Staff would feel involved in the project and therefore have some degree of ownership over and commitment to it. The issue here was that in this large and dispersed faculty, with a large number of staff involved, even coordinating times and venues for focus groups would have been difficult and time-consuming. A compromise might have been to combine a small number of medium-sized focus groups with the survey, providing quantitative as well as qualitative data. It would also have overcome the criticism that it is in the interests of one person responsible for returning for each area to report that everything is fine, whether that is in fact the case, or not. So interviewing more of the staff actually teaching the subjects, and some of the students taking the subjects, to check that what was being claimed actually did happen, would have strengthened the baseline. Such multiple perspectives would have provided a truer picture. All that having been said, the survey approach worked well in terms of getting the project going, and staff were free to comment on the process at any time.

Another interesting issue relates to the way in which the generic skills were collapsed into six groups. When Bill reported the project's progress to the Deans' Committee, there was much interest and discussion on this. Were the groupings workable? Did they mean that the other skills were not the responsibility of the departments who were not allocated them? The view of the committee was that, of course, all departments would include all relevant skills, as they had previously. However, the responsibility for explicit teaching and assessment at the introductory level would remain with the designated department.

One view was that, in order for skills to be transferable to new situations, students should have experience of these skills in a range of situations, and the teaching should encourage reflection and the development of metacognition. Consequently, the committee accepted the view that the teaching should incorporate reflection and that being 'generic' by definition means that such skills do not pertain only to particular subjects and students, but should be encouraged in other subjects as well. On the other hand, we needed to limit the skill definitions to what we could actually teach and assess. Perhaps there needed to be scaffolding in the teaching to encourage this, and this could have become part of the staff training that would emanate from the project.

Linked with this was the vital issue of support for students in their learning, even when a systematic, faculty-based programme was in operation. It also raised questions concerning the role of the learning adviser in the process of major curriculum change. For example, learning skills advisers can operate from a central institutional position, advising students from all faculties. A major disadvantage of this approach is that the programmes developed tend to be general in nature, and it is questionable whether students transfer such learning strategies. There are also questions relating to the depth of an appreciation of the peculiarities of the discipline, and the departments within the discipline, that a 'generic' learning adviser can develop. Depth underpins the ability to tease out and explain to students assumptions and expectations. Thus, the location of learning advisory staff in faculties, at the 'coal face' of students' learning, seems to offer some advantages. It is also easier to integrate learning support programmes into mainstream teaching, avoiding the need for a large number of individual consultations where the same information may be repeated many times. Furthermore, students may tend to see accessing such programmes less as 'remedial', and as just a normal part of the operation of the faculty.

Explicit attention in a systematic way to skills development in the curriculum is a boon to many students. For international students, whose educational backgrounds may have had a different focus, and for mature aged students who have been away from education for some time, explicit instruction and focus can help support transition into university study. Contingent on this is the support that academic staff give to the project in their teaching. It is one thing to tell staff that something must be done, and another for it to be done in a way that is supportive and enthusiastic, conveying to students that what they are learning is important in their university studies and that more than lip service will be paid to it.

The next step is developing the materials and services for students found wanting at the basic level. Perhaps a comprehensive and well designed range will help staff feel supported in the project and implicitly emphasize its importance. It will also mean that learning skills staff can operate in a truly integrated way, bringing their considerable and close knowledge of student learning to bear on the development of resources.

CHAPTER 20

THE GOLDEN TRIANGLE

Case reporter: Phillipa Ferst

Issues raised

This case concerns dilemmas that learning support tutors face in the triangular relationship comprising themselves, students and subject tutors.

Background

The incident in this case occurred at an English university college that facilitates the higher education of students from a range of widely diverse social and academic backgrounds. A considerable proportion of the students were of mature age. Sadie, the student in the case, was 40 years old and was being supported by the learning support tutor who was at the time 51 years old and had been teaching for 23 years, but had only been supporting English native speakers' learning development for six months.

PART 1

I was thrilled to get the chance to help native English speakers with their study skills. Until then, I had been an ESL (English as a second language) lecturer. Although I loved teaching foreign students, the idea of a change and a challenge appealed to me. The interesting student mix at the college, including both home and overseas, young and old students, would enhance my professional development.

Of course, I had read up on theories and models of learning support. From this, I deduced that being a support tutor would allow me to give feedback to students and echo subject tutors' feedback, without playing the role of assessor myself. I had learnt about the 'triangle of support': the student, subject tutor and myself – the learning support tutor. Enthusiastically, I tried to apply the guidelines I had learnt about in my one to one support sessions. 'Be discreet,' I was told, 'listen carefully, and don't do the students' papers for them.'

One autumn afternoon, Sadie came to see me. She was a mature aged Scottish student in the final year of her degree course. Her manner was rather subdued and it was obvious that she lacked self-esteem. I chatted to her for a few minutes, as this usually puts students at ease and helps me to gain insight into their needs. We decided to focus on time management and essay writing, as these were areas in which her dyslexia caused great problems. According to feedback from her subject tutor, Mike Wells, Sadie's main difficulties lay with essay structure, grammatical expression, spelling and punctuation. Generally, Mike gave her low passes for her assignments. However, his feedback comments were constructive and he praised her research skills and her content. He commented that learning support might assist her to raise her grades.

Sadie consulted me on a regular basis as the autumn term progressed. I thought that she regarded me as a friendly and supportive adviser. From the advice I gave her about her marked written work, she noted down tips and strategies on organizing her written work and making it flow. I also gained insight into her learning style and her writing process. Certainly she had little confidence in her own ability. 'I haven't written an essay since I was at school,' she confided. 'And even then my writing was rubbish, although one teacher did say I had a vivid imagination.' But Sadie persevered, drafting and redrafting her work. I encouraged her and was enthusiastic about the potential for improvement. I could see that her ideas were fresh and original. I could also see that she badly needed her confidence boosting, so as the sessions continued I encouraged her to view feedback constructively, to be kind to herself and her writing.

Sadie started to progress gradually. This was reflected in higher grades for her written work and encouraging feedback from her subject tutor. We had developed a good rapport and often joked in a way that made her more relaxed. This rapport seemed closer because of our commonalities, both of us being women and mothers. I had also spent part of my life in the same area of Scotland as Sadie. It gradually emerged that Sadie was stressed because of circumstances outside college. Her husband was unemployed and resented the time she spent on her studies. She had three demanding children and a part-time job. Yet as her college work improved, she began to feel more positive and self-confident. Unfortunately, these feelings were to be short-lived.

I saw almost nothing of Sadie during the second term. Wrongly, I concluded that all was going well. Then one afternoon she booked an appointment to see me. When I looked back, all the signs were staring me in the face, but somehow I missed them. Sadie was downcast. 'I've got a new tutor now for this term's module – Mr Barton,' she said. 'And he only gave me 30 per cent (a fail) after I worked so hard on this,' she sighed. 'Just look at the comments. They're awful!'

I did, and they were, but I had to be diplomatic. Certainly, there were rather a lot of negative comments and, worse still, they were worded in a way that would have infuriated me had it been my essay. 'Appalling grammar', 'What on earth does this mean?' 'Is this a sentence?' and other such remarks peppered the text. Red circles pinpointed the errors. I had never seen such emphasis on transcriptional errors. Few comments had been made about the content, except 'I cannot agree with you here'. I took a deep breath. After all, Richard Barton must have had specific expectations of the essay which had not been fulfilled and besides, I reasoned, evaluation was his concern, not mine. 'Maybe, he's just a stricter marker. Markers differ so much,' I said, hating myself. 'We can do more work on your grammar anyway.' I looked through the essay some more. 'Wow – your linking words are a bit better. You've used some of those I suggested last time.' Sadie's eyes glistened with tears. 'I'm glad *something* is OK. I felt I was doing so well.' We chatted some more, then she said she ought to go, as one of the kids was ill.

No warning bells sounded for me at that time. I felt her disappointment very keenly, but after all, essays could be a matter of luck and one had to be prepared for ups and downs in studying. Meanwhile, other students came for support and the term drew to an end. In the next few weeks, no appointments were made for me to see Sadie. I concluded that things were on an even keel.

Then out of the blue came the desperate summons to duty – a call that was to test both my temper and my talents. I had just finished my last afternoon session when my boss came in and announced that I was urgently needed down the corridor. 'You know Sadie, don't you?' he said. 'She is in a bit of a state and her personal tutor, Alan Brockman, is in class for the next hour or so. Could you help us out and just sit with her until he comes? It might be quite a time.' Of course I could. I had to.

Loud sobbing came from the office where Sadie was waiting. She was sitting with her head in her hands, weeping uncontrollably. I had to subdue my own emotions and focus my mind on what confronted me. Suddenly, I remembered the advice a colleague had once given me. 'Don't appear too emotional yourself, because it may upset the student more.' Sadie's turmoil had rendered her speechless. She grabbed her pen and wrote on a piece of paper, blotching it with tears as she wrote: 'My tutor (Mr Barton) told me my essay is unreadable because of the bad grammar. He wants me to read it through aloud to him. I just can't. I don't know what to do.'

I felt at a loss about how to respond. I tried to compose myself and conjure up a sense of detachment and objectivity. Sadie then managed to speak. 'He's completely shattered my confidence.' And she began to cry again, loudly and despairingly. Try as I might, tears sprang into my own eyes, tears of distress for the collapse of her hopes and of anger at the painstaking work which we had carried out together. All this had been undone in such a short time and to such disastrous effect. To me, the situation resembled that of Humpty Dumpty after the fall. The pieces were scattered all over the floor.

How would you have reacted in this situation?
What do you think happened next?

PART 2

I decided to subdue my own emotions and then to find some way to distance Sadie from the highly charged situation. I reasoned that however powerful my own feelings were about her treatment, mixing my emotions with hers would only serve to brew a more volatile cocktail. Later, I could ask her to put her feelings on paper. We were used to working together on her writing and she knew that I would respond constructively.

On a practical level, I decided that basic needs were the primary issue and so produced paper tissues and a couple of drinks, while Sadie worked through her emotions. Meanwhile, I tried to figure out a useful approach. Thankfully, out of the urgency of the situation, a memory sprang to mind which drew on my knowledge of Sadie. I told her, 'When I was at school in Scotland, one of the teachers insisted on calling *me* Sadie, because she couldn't pronounce my name.' Sadie smiled.

I then went on to tell her funny things that had happened when I lived in Scotland, like the rabbits I had bought, which turned out too old to breed from, and so on. Gradually, because the topic was unrelated to Sadie's situation, she stopped sobbing and I could see that she was getting back to normal. Her sense of humour rose to the surface as we shared experiences that were positive instead of negative.

I sensed that she was now calm enough to list possible courses of action that she could take and then show these to her personal tutor. She made two headings: action she could take right away and longer-term actions. She relaxed as she became absorbed in writing. Under the first heading, we negotiated what she would write for her personal tutor, and I agreed to let him know before he saw her, in case repeating her story upset her.

Her short-term points were to ask her personal tutor to help her change her current subject tutor and to book another appointment to see me. As Sadie said, the praise that is so important in teaching and learning was missing for her. She wanted 'a new start'. She also stressed that she did not want to cause any trouble, but she needed to 'survive' and get through the course.

Her long-term points were to work on her time management in order to give herself a chance to relax, and to reflect on her studies and to visit the Support Unit regularly to improve her written work. This and the help given by her personal tutor were important sources of strength for her. When, soon afterwards, Sadie's personal tutor arrived, I gave him an update on what had occurred and left Sadie to his care.

What do you think of the course of action taken by the learning support person?
Do you think the learning support person should have confronted the subject tutor?

CASE REPORTER'S DISCUSSION

It could easily be argued that there are implications for further action in this case, such as contacting the subject tutor concerned or conducting an investigation into the matter. But Sadie had made no complaint against the tutor. In fact she had accepted the negative feedback, but this had increased her apprehension about writing and confirmed her doubts about her academic ability.

More importantly, the issue of confidentiality was in question. The Support Unit encourages tutors to recommend students who need academic support, but it also respects confidentiality. So, it is important to keep the trust of both students and staff, while encouraging staff to help their students make the most of the support facilities. This has implications for communications both between the college teaching departments and the Study Support Unit, and inside departments themselves. Sadie had improved her essay grades after going to the Support Unit and her previous tutor, Mike Wells, knew this. But somehow, the new tutor, Mr Barton, had not been aware of this improvement and had not given Sadie any credit for her hard work.

I felt that I had acted positively in the circumstances. First of all, I was glad I'd been there to help Sadie, as she needed someone friendly and whom she trusted. I think it was important to spend the time calming her down before trying to tackle the problems. It was also useful to write things down, and this worked in Sadie's situation. In fact the points she wrote helped her to distance herself (and me) from the person who had caused the friction. It meant that issues of confidentiality could be observed.

The actual incident, which lasted about an hour and a half, was traumatic. But in the end, both of us were triumphant as we worked through the problems together. There might still be future problems, but this approach proved to be a successful first step for Sadie. It helped her to climb back to where she was before, and hopefully that journey will continue. In fact the story did have a happy ending, as I attended Sadie's degree ceremony that summer. There, she took the opportunity to say how pleased she was with her achievement and with the help that she had received.

For me, the incident raised issues of ways to proactively deal with such situations. A strength that emerged from it was that it motivated me to research and develop. Six months after the incident, I presented a college workshop on feedback on student writing, attracting a wide range of staff. I included a task in which staff were asked to give written feedback on an essay extract. It was surprising to me how many of them were negative in their feedback, both in what they wrote and how they wrote it. They responded like judges, not 'consultants' as Zamel (1985: 97) recommends. This spurred me on to research the role of the support tutor in feedback on student writing.

Some time after the incident, I asked Sadie out of curiosity what she now thought about it. She replied, 'Oh, that seems so long ago. I've gotten over it. I am stronger. I won't let people walk over me now.' I asked her whether she would lend me that old essay to use for the conference and she agreed. 'Anything to help other students not go through what I did,' she said.

During my conference paper, I circulated copies of the retyped essay, minus feedback, for participants to comment on and grade. Interestingly, it received a reasonable pass, not a fail as before. I then passed round the original (anonymous) retyped feedback comments. They drew appalled reactions from the audience. 'The ideas are so good – why attack the grammar and style so much?' was one comment. Why indeed? But then the standard of written (or spoken) English of mature students from disadvantaged backgrounds is sometimes regarded by middle class tutors as fair game. After all, it is far easier to pinpoint transcriptional errors than it is to evaluate ideas.

I think that the incident in this case study was a turning point for me as a study support tutor as well as for Sadie, the student I supported. I feel pleased with the action that I took and see it as a learning experience for both myself and Sadie. It spurred me to act proactively and in a systematic way about difficulties I encountered between students and their teachers, while at the same time retaining confidentiality. Today, I am even more aware of the important and responsible role that I have as support tutor. I am not a gate-keeper, so I inspire the students' trust. Also, I am not an expert in their field of study, and this may put the relationships on a more equal footing.

The position of the support tutor can be a tricky one, as in the dilemma outlined. Certainly, there is bonding between the student and the support tutor, who must keep a cool head when he or she interprets written feedback. So compromise is always on the agenda and it is a question of the balance between helping the student and standing back.

Helping mature aged students who are experiencing learning difficulties involves a high degree of sympathy, and this is what I was able to provide for Sadie. Tutors need to remember that such students may have problems coping with academic genres and may need assistance to tease out the particular ways of thinking that underpin them. Furthermore, achievement is hard won for such students, and they need plenty of support. But those who offer support must work together with subject staff in an atmosphere of trust. Perhaps this will lead to the development of a sense of community within higher education, one where tutors reflect on their attitude to feedback, particularly regarding mature students. So the triangle of support, which involves me, the student and the subject teacher does not have to be an 'uneasy' triangle: it can be an empowering and a 'golden' triangle.

Reference

Zamel, V (1985) Responding to student writing, *Tesol Quarterly*, **19** (March), p 95

CONCLUSION

CHAPTER 21

DIMENSIONS OF STUDENT LEARNING SUPPORT

Glenda Crosling and Graham Webb

In Chapter 1 we discussed the rapidly-changing higher education context and the important role that student learning support has come to play within this. We commented on the diversity of the student population, the consequent need for support programmes to be wide-ranging, and the multi-faceted activity of learning support providers.

The variety of contexts and forms of support provision is strikingly evident in the cases. They provide a rich environment within which the problems, issues and crises of students, subject teachers and learning support staff are played out. But while the responses are unique and unpredictable in many ways, it is possible to suggest some recurring themes and issues that emerge from the cases. In this concluding chapter we attempt to identify these themes and issues. To some extent, almost every theme occurs in every case, but we have attempted to classify cases in terms of the major one or two themes that they represent. The major themes or issues we identify in terms of student and then staff issues are as follows.

Relating to students

- Rapport and trust;
- confidence and motivation;
- empowerment;
- objectivity;
- communication.

Relating to staff

- Working with subject teachers;
- integration in the curriculum;
- the teaching of support programmes.

ISSUES RELATING TO STUDENTS

Rapport and trust

Many of the cases emphasize the importance of building rapport and trust with students. There are compelling accounts of disillusioned, emotional and distraught students in the cases, which emphasize the crucial nature of the relationship between students and learning supporters. This is expressed poignantly in 'The heart and the machine' (Chapter 2) and 'The golden triangle' (Chapter 20). In 'Back on course – but...' (Chapter 14), the fundamental importance of trust is illustrated as a student is pushed close to the edge by her dyslexia. In 'Mentoring Rosie' (Chapter 1), a bridge is built by the learning supporter's disclosure of similar experiences to the student from a non-traditional cultural, linguistic and social background, and this is also the situation in 'The golden triangle', where there are shared childhood experiences.

Confidence and motivation

Building on rapport and trust, several cases demonstrate the importance of developing students' confidence and motivation as a basis for success. In 'I can only do it with aspirin' (Chapter 9), these aspects are addressed in pre-course workshops to develop nursing students' mathematical skills and approaches to study. Confidence and motivation are nurtured by modelling and working with a student as she develops computer skills in 'The heart and the machine' (Chapter 2). They are also cultivated through consciousness-raising programmes, such as the Summer bridging programme, for students whose ethnic and socio-economic backgrounds have not prepared them for higher education study in 'Barriers or bridges?' (Chapter 15). In 'Mentoring Rosie', the mentor provides advice on university services, as well as motivating Rosie by assisting her to choose courses and subjects appropriate to her career goal. Providing specialist advice on appropriate learning approaches proved to be a vital element in increasing confidence and motivation for the student suffering from dyslexia in 'Back on course – but...'. In 'Reading for life' (Chapter 13), confidence and motivation in reading are fostered by taking students to a local library with a friendly atmosphere.

Empowerment

Many of the cases express the limits to the support that can be provided. In fact, in some ways, the existence of support programmes in higher education seems at odds with the independence and self-reliance inherent in higher education study and expected of students. The objective of programmes is therefore to empower students rather than inadvertently to encourage dependence on learning support staff. In 'Accounting: I can do that' (Chapter 10), the author explicitly broaches the issue of when support becomes 'mollycoddling' in assisting students from a course with a very high failure rate. This is also a theme in 'Freedom to fail' (Chapter 6), where the teacher's endeavours to bridge the gap between adolescence and adulthood, in order to assist a student to work independently and reliably, are perceived by the student as interfering with his independence. This proves to be a learning experience for the subject teacher as she contemplates the limits of her role. The issue for the learning supporter in 'Dilemma for two' (Chapter 8), in working through a number of complex issues, is whether there is a need to inform police, parents or tutors of an alleged criminal activity. In 'Reading for life' (Chapter 13) students are empowered to think creatively and critically about texts by facilitating their engagement with them.

An interesting example of empowerment is seen in 'Taking the initiative' (Chapter 16) when an overseas student with poor English language skills empowers herself to complete a PhD in record time. Other examples of empowerment can be found in 'Letter of the law' (Chapter 17), 'I can only do it with aspirin' (Chapter 9), 'Barriers or bridges?' (Cchapter 15), 'What's information literacy?' (Chapter 11), 'How can we reach them?' (Chapter 12), and 'Reading for life' (Chapter 13).

Objectivity

Intertwined in the student–learning supporter relationship is the need to adopt an objective and non-judgemental approach. Learning supporters try to balance the needs of the students with the demands of the higher education system, as well as with their own prejudices and preferences. In 'Doing it hard' (Chapter 3), the situation is acute, with teachers having to put to one side their own abhorrence of the acts and behaviour of the student, who is also a prisoner. In 'Dilemma for two' (Chapter 8), the support provider has to decide on the authenticity of the student's plea for a letter seeking special exam consideration.

Communication

A significant aspect of the learning supporter's role is communication with students. Several cases demonstrate the opportunity for miscommunication with students from different language and cultural backgrounds. What emerges from these cases is the alarming ease with which cross-cultural miscommunication can occur, whether through misinterpretation of body language, as in 'Intercultural inexperience' (Chapter 5), or through social and emotional misinterpretation of intention in electronic communications as in 'Lovely ShirLey' (Chapter 7). On the other hand, in 'Freedom to fail' (Chapter 6), the teacher sees e-mail communication as a way for staff to communicate with students more effectively. Miscommunication based on differing value systems and expectations is evident in 'The personal is the professional' (Chapter 4), not only between the teachers and the students, but also among groups of students, including gay and lesbian students. The use of vernacular rather than Standard English is a feature of 'Accounting: I can do that' (Chapter 10), as the teacher tries to facilitate a sense of comfort and understanding of difficult concepts.

ISSUES RELATING TO STAFF

Working with subject teachers

The importance of a collaborative relationship between the subject teacher and learning supporter is demonstrated in 'Letter of the law' (Chapter 17) and 'Accounting: I can do that' (Chapter 10). In 'Academic friend or foe?' (Chapter 18), it is through the learning supporter's relationship with a subject teacher in a difficult environment at a rural campus that student learning is enhanced. By contrast, in 'The heart and the machine' (Chapter 2), the policy of the support unit is that staff development is not really the responsibility of the unit, and in this case the author reflects on whether she could have supported the teacher as well as the student.

A broader perspective of working with teaching staff is investigated in 'Generalizing the generic' (Chapter 19), through the explicit focus on generic skills across the curriculum of a large faculty. An important aspect of this process is the need to gain the cooperation and support of staff, and ways to involve staff are considered. In 'What's information literacy?' (Chapter 11), it is through a collaborative teaching approach with library staff that the subject teachers are also able to develop their own information literacy skills. The activities and approaches used in the support programme in 'Letter of the law' (Chapter 17) are built on the materials and guidance provided by the subject teacher.

Integration in the curriculum

'Letter of the law' also provides a good example of how learning the language and discourse of law is addressed by integrating this learning within the content of a commerce degree. In 'Mentoring Rosie' (Chapter 1), a student is encouraged to attend a writing centre which operates concurrently with the student's courses. In 'What's information literacy?' (Chapter 11), the teaching of information literacy skills is interwoven with the teaching of the subject content, to the point that an assignment could not be completed without students utilizing such skills. And in 'How can we reach them?' (Chapter 12), electronic online delivery is seen as the optimum way to support students academically in an undergraduate engineering course.

In some cases, integration occurs in terms of preparation for study. In 'Barriers or bridges?' (Chapter 15), the Talent Search and Upward Bound programmes operate while students are at secondary school. The case 'I can only do it with aspirin' (Chapter 9) discusses a mathematics course for beginning nursing students which proactively endeavours to assist students' transition to their studies through developing skills that may be lacking.

The cases 'Back on course – but...' (Chapter 14) and 'Dilemma for two' (Chapter 8) revolve around services that are vital to, but a little removed from, direct academic support. In 'Back on course – but...', a dyslexic support service external to the higher education institution is drawn upon, whereas in 'Dilemma for two' the institution's counselling service provides support. Other cases displaying integration of learning support in the curriculum include 'Academic friend or foe?' (Chapter 18), 'Generalizing the generic' (Chapter 19) and 'What's information literacy?' (Chapter 11).

The teaching of support programmes

The teaching or delivery of learning support programmes is explored in many of the cases. In 'I can only do it with aspirin' (Chapter 9), the resistance of some students to the teaching approach requires the teacher to acknowledge students' differing learning styles and needs. 'Freedom to fail' (Chapter 6) emphasizes the initial transition that students need to make to the independence expected of them in higher education, and the effect that limited support during transition can have on a student's academic performance. The importance of student to student and tutor to student interaction in teaching is elaborated in 'Accounting: I can do that' (Chapter 10), and 'What's information literacy?' (Chapter 11). 'The heart and the machine' (Chapter 2) and 'Reading for life' (Chapter 13) are cases where the value of modelling by the support programme providers is a vehicle to promote learning.

Several cases consider students' learning styles. In 'How can we reach them?' (Chapter 12) the students' interest and affinity with online communication and learning is acknowledged and utilized for delivery of the support programme. A clash over learning styles in 'Reading for life' (Chapter 13) is overcome as students begin to see the benefits of the approach taken by the teachers. The case 'Back on course – but...' (Chapter 14) presents modes of learning that suit the needs of a student with dyslexia. In 'What's information

literacy?' (Chapter 11) students at a distance are able to use video conferencing and videotapes, as well as e-mail and voice-mail, to communicate with
their teachers.

Finally, interesting teaching approaches are explored in 'Barriers or
bridges?' (Chapter 15), where a constructivist approach is adopted as the
student is encouraged to consider how his experiences have shaped his
perspective, while 'What's information literacy?' (Chapter 11) considers
assessment issues in relation to the development of lifelong learning skills.

Final thoughts

We would like to close by thanking the case authors for contributing what, in
many ways, have been painful and frustrating experiences for them as they
confronted difficulties and sought to provide support for their students. We
also celebrate the creative and thoughtful ways in which they have designed
and delivered their responses. The cases illustrate time and again that
students, their backgrounds and their responses to programmes cannot be
removed from the equation of teaching in higher education. There seems to
be an inescapable conclusion that improvements and solutions can only be
reached when students, subject teachers, curriculum and learning supporters
are all part of the design process. It is also particularly interesting that, in
many cases, it is the learning supporter who provides the leadership and
initiative for this.

We hope that the cases in this book provide both insights and ideas. We
hope they provide useful points for reflection on past experiences and useful
indications to guide future activity. We encourage you to contact the case
authors or ourselves to discuss the cases further, and wish you every success in
your learning support endeavours.

FURTHER READING

Beasley, C J (1990) Content-based language instruction: helping ESL/EFL students with language and study skills at tertiary level, *TESOL in Context*, **1**, pp 10–14

Beasley, C J and Pearson, C A L (1999) Facilitating the learning of transitional students: strategies for success for all students, *Higher Education Research and Development*, **18**, pp 303–21

Boero, P (1999) Teaching and learning mathematics in context, *Educational Studies in Mathematics*, **39** (1–3)

Buzan, T (1993) *The Mind Map Book: Radiant thinking*, BBC, London

Casanave, C P (1998) Transitions: the balancing act of bilingual academics, *Journal of Second Language Writing*, **7** (2)

Casazza, M and Silverman, S (1996) *Learning Assistance and Developmental Education*, Jossey-Bass, San Francisco

Chi, F M (1995) *Discussion as Inquiry in ESL/EFL Reading: A study of Taiwanese college students' meaning-construction of a literary text through small group discussion*, paper presented at the Annual Meeting of the Teachers of English to Speakers of Other Languages

Cohen, L J (1992) *Bibliotherapy: The experience of therapeutic reading from the perspective of the adult reader*, Michigan University Press, Ann Arbor, Mich.

Cotesta, P, Crosling, G and Murphy, H (1998) *Writing for Accounting Students*, Butterworths, Sydney

Cottrell, S (1999) *The Study Skills Handbook: Macmillan study guides*, Macmillan, London

Crosling, G (1996a) Multi level structure of meaning in a business law tutorial, *Australian Review of Applied Linguistics*, **19** (1), pp 91–111

Crosling, G (1996b) International students writing in English: improvement through transition, *Prospect: A Journal of Australian TESOL*, **11** (1), pp 50–58

Crosling, G M and Murphy, H M (2000) *How to Study Business Law: Reading, writing and exams*, 3rd edn, Butterworths, Sydney

Crosling, G and Ward, I (2000) Transition to university: the role of oral communication in the undergraduate curriculum, *Journal Of Institutional Research*, **9** (1)

Daniels, H (1994) *Literature Circles: Voice and choice in the student-centered classroom*, Pembroke, Ontario

De Porter, B (1993) *Quantum Learning*, Piatkus, London

Earwaker, J (1992) *Helping and Supporting Students*, Society for Research into Higher Education and Open University Press, Buckingham

Evans, J (1999) Building bridges: reflecting on the problems of transfer of learning in mathematics, *Educational Studies in Mathematics*, **39**, pp 23–44

Fitzgerald, J, Garcia, G E, Jimenez, R T and Barrera, R (2000) How will bilingual/ESL programs in literacy change in the next millennium?, *Reading Research Quarterly*, **35** (4), pp 520–23

Flippo, R and Caverly, D (2000) *Handbook of College Reading and Study Strategy Research*, Lawrence Erlbaum Associates, Mahwah, NJ

Gaff, J, Ratcliff, J and Associates (1996) *Handbook for the Undergraduate Curriculum*, Jossey-Bass, San Francisco

Gains, J (1999) Electronic mail – a new style of communication or just a new medium? An investigation into the text features of email, *English for Specific Purposes*, 18 (1), pp 81–101

Gonzalez, O (1999) Building vocabulary: dictionary consultation and the ESL student, *Journal of Adolescent and Adult Literacy*, 43 (3), pp 264–71

Harklau, L, Losey, K and Siegal, M (1999) *Generation 1.5 Meets College Composition*, Lawrence Erlbaum, Mahwah, NJ

Hetherington, J (1996) Approaches to the development of self esteem in dyslexic students, in *Conference Proceedings: Dyslexic students in higher education, practical responses to student and institutional needs*, SKILL/University of Huddersfield

Hoyles, C, Noss, R and Pozzi, S (1999) Mathematizing in practice, in *Studies in Mathematics Education Series*, vol 10, ed C Hoyles, C Morgan and G Woodhouse, pp 48–62, Falmer Press, London

Inner London Probation Service (1993) *Working With Difference: A positive and practical guide to anti-discriminatory practice teaching*, Inner London Probation Service, London

Ivanic, R (1998) *Writing and Identity*, John Benjamins, Amsterdam

Kendon, A (1999) The negotiation of context in face-to-face interaction, in *Rethinking Context: Language as an interactive phenomenon*, ed A Durante and C Goodwin, pp 323–35, Cambridge University Press, Cambridge

Kortz, W (2001) Computers as a second language: for teachers too!, *Learning Technology*, **3** (1) [Online] http://www.usm.maine.edu/com/lindap1.htm

Lawrence, C, Kavanagh, L, McLean, P, Logan, M, Thompson, G and Curmi, H (2001) *Staying Sane on Campus: Tips and techniques*, Equity and Learning Program at University of Melbourne, Melbourne

Lazar, G (1993) *Literature and Language Teaching: A guide for teachers and trainers*, Cambridge University Press, Cambridge

Lea, M and Stierer, B (2000) *Student Writing in Higher Education*, Society for Research into Higher Education/Open University Press, Buckingham

Leki, I (1992) *Understanding ESL Writers: A guide for teachers*, Boynton-Cook, Portsmouth

Lissner, L S (1990) The learning centre from 1829 to the year 2000 and beyond, in *Handbook of Developmental Education*, ed R M Hashway, Praeger, New York

Lundeberg, M A (1987) Metacognitive aspects of reading comprehension: studying understanding in legal case analysis, *Reading Research Quarterly*, 22, pp 407–32

McGrath, D and Spear, M (1987) The politics of remediation, in *Teaching the Developmental Education Student*, ed K M Ahrendt, New Directors for Community Colleges, no 57, Jossey-Bass, San Francisco

McGrath, D and Townsend, B (1996) Strengthening the preparedness of at risk students, in *Handbook of the Undergraduate Curriculum*, ed J Gaff and J Ratcliff, Jossey-Bass, San Francisco

McInnes, C (2001) Researching the first year experience, *Higher Education Research and Development*, **20** (2)

McInnes, C and James, R (1995) *First Year on Campus*, Australian Government Publishing Service, Canberra

McLean, P, Surtie, F, Elphinstone, L and Devlin, M (1995) Models of learning support in Victorian universities: issues and implications, *Higher Education Research and Development*, **14** (1) pp 75–86

McLoughlan, D, Fitzgibbon, G and Young, V (1994) *Adult Dyslexia: Assessment, counselling and training*, Whurr, London

Morgan, E (no date) *Computer Anxiety: A survey of computer training, experience, anxiety, and administrative support among teachers* [Online] http://www.biochem.okstate.edu/oas/OJAS/amorg

Morgan, E (1995) Releasing potential in the dyslexic writer, *RAPAL Bulletin*, **27**

Moss, W and Cairncross, T (1995) *Students with Specific Learning Difficulties: A research report*, Goldsmiths College, University of London, London

Murphy, H, Crosling, G and Webb, J (1996) Evaluation of language and learning programs: promoting academic credibility, in *Academic Skills Advising: Towards a discipline*, ed M Garner, K Chanock and R Clerehan, Language and Learning Network, Caulfield, Australia

Naiman, N, Frohlich, M, Stern, H and Todesco, A (1978) *The Good Language Learner,* Ontario Institute for Studies in Education, Toronto

National Youth Agency (1999) *Briefing Paper: Lesbian gay and bisexual young people,* National Youth Agency, Leicester

National Youth Agency (1999) *Briefing Paper: Tackling heterosexism and homophobia,* National Youth Agency, Leicester

Orr, L (no date) *Computer Anxiety* [Online] http://lttf.ieee.org/learn_tech/issues/january2001/index.html

Oxford, R (1990) *Language Learning Strategies,* Hienle and Hienle, Boston, Mass.

Pozzi, S, Noss, R and Hoyles, C (1998) Tools in practice, mathematics in use, *Educational Studies in Mathematics,* **36**, pp 105–22

Richards, V, Jurgensen, K and Young, V (1999) How can we do what we do better: towards a model of collegial 'supervision' for practitioners of learning development, in *Getting Together: Learning support and development conference,* ed M Selman Brown, Tertiary Learning Centres in Aotearoa/New Zealand (TLCANZ) Conference Proceedings, **4**, pp 31–39

Robinson, R D, McKenna, M C and Wedman, J M (2000) *Issues and Trends in Literacy Education,* 2nd edn, Allyn and Bacon, Neehman Heights, Mass.

Rosenblatt, L (1978) *The Reader, the Text, the Poem: The transactional theory of the literary work,* Southern Illinois University Press, Carbondale, Ill.

Ruben, J (1975) What the good learner can teach us, *TESOL Quarterly,* **9**, pp 41–51

Ryan, Y and Zuber-Skerritt, O (eds) (1999) *Supervising Postgraduate Students from Non-English-Speaking Backgrounds,* Open University Press, Buckingham

Safford, K (2000) Algebra for adult students: the student voices, in *Perspectives on Adults Learning Mathematics,* ed D Coben, J O'Donoghue and G FitzSimons, Kluwer Academic, Dordrecht

Shaw, P (1991) Science research students' composing processes, *English for Specific Purposes,* **10** (3), pp 189–206

Singleton, C (1999) *Dyslexia in Higher Education: Policy, provision and practice,* University of Hull, National Working Party on Dyslexia in Higher Education, Higher Education Funding Council, Hull

Stacey, G (1997) A dyslexic mind a-thinking, *Dyslexia, Journal of the British Dyslexia Association,* **3** (2)

State University of New York Council of Library Directors (1997) *SUNY CLD Information Literacy Initiative: Final report* [Online] http://olis.sysadm.suny.edu/ili/finalÿ.htm

Steffert, B (1999) Visual spatial ability and dyslexia, part 1 pp 8–49 and part 2 pp 127–67, in *Visual Spatial Ability and Dyslexia,* ed I Padgett, Central St Martins College of Art and Design, London Institute, London

Steinberg, D L, Epstein D and Johnson, R (1997) *Border Patrols: Policing the boundaries of heterosexuality*, Cassell, London

Swales, J (1993) *Genre Analysis*, Cambridge University Press, Cambridge

Swales, J and Feak, C (1994) *Academic Writing for Graduate Students*, University of Michigan Press, Michigan

Tompkins, G E and McGee, L M (1993) *Teaching Reading with Literature: Case studies to action plans*, Macmillan, New York

Vance, S and Crosling, G (1998) Integrating writing with the curriculum: a social constructionist approach, in *University Teaching: International Perspectives*, ed J F Forest, Garland Studies in Higher Education, vol 13, Garland, Boston, Mass.

Vinegrad, M (1994) *Dyslexia at College: A practical study*, Educare, London

Webb, G (1996) *Understanding Staff Development*, Society for Research into Higher Education/Open University Press, Buckingham

Webb, J (2001) Using the web to explore issues related to the first year experience, *Higher Education Research and Development*, **20** (2), pp 225–36

West, T G (1997) *In the Mind's Eye*, Bantam, New York

Wheeler, S and Birtle, J (1993) *A Handbook for Personal Tutors*, Society for Research into Higher Education and Open University Press, Buckingham

Williams, L (1983) *Teaching for the Two Sided Mind*, Simon and Schuster, New York

Worrell, P (1990) Metacognition: implications for instruction in nursing education, *Journal of Nursing Education*, **29** (4), pp 170–75

Yerbury, H and Kirk, J (1990) Questions of professional practice: innovation in the education of information professionals, in *The Changing Face of Professional Education*, ed M Bezzina and J Butcher, AARE, Sydney

Zigouras, C (1999) Cultural diversity and transnational delivery, in *Responding to Diversity, Proceedings from the 16th Annual Conference of the Australasian Society for Computers in Learning in Tertiary Education*, ed J Winn, pp 401–7, University of Queensland, Brisbane

Index

academic
  reading 7, 111–18, 139
  writing 6, 20, 94, 106, 107,
      123, 138, 145, 149, 171
academic staff relationships with
      support providers 26, 28, 31,
      91, 95, 105, 147, 148, 151,
      153–61, 170–76
accounting 81
advice, course in 22, 36
assessment, student 50, 58, 62,
      89, 99, 101, 105, 115, 121,
      145, 172, 175
attitudes, teaching 1, 34, 38, 46,
      50, 65, 97, 102, 130, 154, 167

body language, teaching 49, 52,
      53

changes, in higher education 1
Chinese background students 50
communication
  body language 49, 52, 53
  conflict resolution in 54
  course 49
  e-mail 58, 61, 62, 64, 64–71
  intercultural 49–56, 53, 55, 64,
      93
community and youth studies 41
computers 25
confidentiality 72, 73, 76, 77

conflict resolution 54
constructivist approach 131, 132
consultations
  individual 25
contextualising, support programs
      4, 5, 6, 86, 93, 104, 105,
      145–52, 150, 158, 159
course
  accounting 81
  advice 22, 36
  community and youth studies
      41
  computers 25
  creative arts 25
  nursing 82
counselling services 21, 28, 30,
      63, 67
creative arts 25
criminal activity 74
crises, teaching 1

disadvantaged students 111, 113,
      146, 150, 163
discrimination 41, 43, 45, 47
diversity of backgrounds, students'
      1, 3, 9, 18, 21, 41, 57, 97, 145,
      164
dyslexia 119, 125

e-mail 58, 61, 62, 64, 64–71

English language   111–13, 116, 117, 126, 134, 141, 146, 151
evaluation, support programs   43, 46, 47

failing   1, 128

generic skills/lifelong learning, support for   2, 162–69

higher education
   changes in   1
   massification   1, 2
   transition to   3, 6, 57, 96
history, support programs   2
immigrant students   18, 50, 64, 126
individual consultations   25
intercultural communication   49–56, 53, 55, 64, 93

learning, students'
   emotional issues in   4, 25, 30, 44, 58, 61, 69, 83, 84, 101, 120, 128, 134–42
   constructivist *see* teaching, in support programs
   styles of   122, 123, 124, 131, 155
location, support providers   168

massification, higher education   1, 2
mathematics support program   81–87
mature aged students   26, 31, 65
mentoring   17–24, 90, 97
modelling, in support programs   29, 99

non-traditional backgrounds, students from   2
nursing   26

online courses, support programs   2, 3, 106, 108
overseas students   26, 29

personal problems, students with   73
plagiarism   140
postgraduate students   111, 134
pre-course acquaintance/bridging courses   3, 82, 89, 127, 128, 135

reading, academic   7, 111–18, 139
relationships
   confidentiality and ethics   72, 76, 77
   exams   73, 76
   social distance   26, 29, 71
   with students (empathy)   19, 21, 22, 25, 28, 30, 37, 81, 173
   with academic staff   26, 28, 31, 91, 95, 105, 147, 148, 151, 153–61, 170–76

school leaver students   63
services, counselling   21, 28, 30, 63, 67
social distance, support providers and students   26, 29, 71
stress, students and staff   20, 27, 115, 119, 121, 128, 140, 172
students'
   assessment   50, 58, 62, 89, 99, 101, 105, 115, 121, 145, 172, 175
   criminal activity   74
   emotional issues in learning   4, 25, 30, 44, 58, 61, 69, 83, 84, 101, 120, 128, 134–42
   diversity of backgrounds   1, 3, 9, 18, 21, 41, 57, 97, 145, 164
   Chinese students   50
   disadvantaged   111, 134, 146, 150, 163

immigrant 18, 50, 64, 126
in prison 34–40, 35
mature aged 26, 31, 65
non-traditional 2
overseas 26, 29
school leavers 63
dyslexia 119, 125
failing 1, 128
gender 22
graduation 37, 40, 174
personal problems 73
postgraduate 111, 134
sexuality 42
success 1, 24, 36, 92
styles of learning 122, 123, 124,
    131, 155
successful students 1, 24, 36, 92
supplemental instruction 3, 88–95
support programs
    academic writing in 6, 20, 94,
        106, 107, 123, 138, 145,
        149, 171
    contextualising of 4, 5, 6, 86,
        93, 104, 105, 145–152, 149,
        150, 158, 159
    discrimination in 41, 43, 45, 47
    evaluation of 43, 46, 47
    history of 2
    generic skills/lifelong learning
        2, 162–69
    mentoring 17–24, 90, 97
    online 2, 3, 106, 108
    pre-course acquaintance/bridging
        3, 82, 89, 127, 128, 135

supplemental instruction 3,
    88–95
support providers
    location of 168
    relationships with students 19,
        21, 22, 25, 28, 30, 37, 81,
        173

teaching
    attitudes 1, 34, 38, 46, 50, 65,
        97, 102, 130, 154, 167,
    body language 49, 52, 53
    constructivist approach 131,
        132
    crises in 1
    for understanding 85, 86, 98
    in support programs
    modelling 29, 99
    value systems 38, 50, 66, 70,
        120, 162
transition to higher education 3,
    6, 57, 96

understanding, in teaching 85, 86,
    98
universities *see* higher education

value systems, in teaching 38, 50,
    66, 70, 120, 162

writing
    academic 6, 20, 94, 106, 107,
        123, 138, 145, 149, 171
    plagiarism *see* main entry